Access to History
General Editor: Keith Randell

Stagnation and Reform: the USSR 1964-91

John Laver

Hodder & Stoughton

A MEMBER OF THE HODDER HEADLINE GROUP

The cover illustration is a photograph of Mikhail Gorbachev, courtesy of Camera Press Ltd.

Some other titles in the series:

Russia 1815-81   ISBN 0 340 54789 8
Russell Sherman

Reactions and Revolutions: Russia 1881-1924   ISBN 0 340 53336 6
Michael Lynch

Stalin and Khrushchev: The USSR 1924-64   ISBN 0 340 53335 8
Michael Lynch

France: The Third Republic 1870-1914   ISBN 0 340 55569 6
Keith Randell

China: From Empire to People's Republic 1900-49   ISBN 0 340 62702 6
Michael Lynch

The People's Republic of China 1949-90   ISBN 0 340 68853 X
Michael Lynch

British Library Cataloguing in Publication Data

A catalogue for this title is available from the British Library

ISBN 0-340-62702-6

First published 1997

Impression number   10 9   8   7   6   5   4   3   2   1
Year   1999   1998   1997

Copyright © 1997 John Laver

Typeset by Sempringham publishing services, Bedford
Printed in Great Britain for Hodder & Stoughton Educational,
a division of Hodder Headline Plc, 338 Euston Road, London NW1 3BH
by Redwood Books, Trowbridge, Wiltshire

Contents

Preface

To the general reader

Although the *Access to History* series has been designed with the needs of students studying the subject at higher examination levels very much in mind, it also has a great deal to offer the general reader. The main body of the text (i.e. ignoring the Study Guides at the ends of chapters) forms a readable and yet stimulating survey of a coherent topic as studied by historians. However, each author's aim has not merely been to provide a clear explanation of what happened in the past (to interest and inform): it has also been assumed that most readers wish to be stimulated into thinking further about the topic and to form opinions of their own about the significance of the events that are described and discussed (to be challenged). Thus, although no prior knowledge of the topic is expected on the reader's part, she or he is treated as an intelligent and thinking person throughout. The author tends to share ideas and possibilities with the reader, rather than passing on numbers of so-called 'historical truths'.

To the student reader

There are many ways in which the series can be used by students studying History at a higher level. It will, therefore, be worthwhile thinking about your own study strategy before you start your work on this book. Obviously, your strategy will vary depending on the aim you have in mind, and the time for study that is available to you.

If, for example, you want to acquire a general overview of the topic in the shortest possible time, the following approach will probably be the most effective:

1 Read Chapter 1 and think about its contents.
2 Read the 'Making notes' section at the end of Chapter 2 and decide whether it is necessary for you to read this chapter.
3 If it is, read the chapter, stopping at each heading to note down the main points that have been made.
4 Repeat stage 2 (and stage 3 where appropriate) for all the other chapters.

If, however, your aim is to gain a thorough grasp of the topic, taking however much time is necessary to do so, you may benefit from carrying out the same procedure with each chapter, as follows:

1 Read the chapter as fast as you can, and preferably at one sitting.
2 Study the flow diagram at the end of the chapter, ensuring that you understand the general 'shape' of what you have just read.

3 Read the 'Making notes' section (and the 'Answering essay questions' section, if there is one) and decide what further work you need to do on the chapter. In particularly important sections of the book, this will involve reading the chapter a second time and stopping at each heading to think about (and to write a summary of) what you have just read.

4 Attempt the 'Source-based questions' section. It will sometimes be sufficient to think through your answers, but additional understanding will often be gained by forcing yourself to write them down.

When you have finished the main chapters of the book, study the 'Further Reading' section and decide what additional reading (if any) you will do on the topic.

This book has been designed to help make your studies both enjoyable and successful. If you can think of ways in which this could have been done more effectively, please write to tell me. In the meantime, I hope that you will gain greatly from your study of History.

Keith Randell

Acknowledgements

The Publishers would like to thank the following for permission to reproduce illustrations in this volume:

Cover - Camera Press Ltd.

Text acknowledgement: Cambridge University Press for the extract from *Gorbachev and After* by Stephen White (1991).

CHAPTER 1

Introduction: The USSR under Brezhnev and Gorbachev - The Life and Death of a Superpower

1 The Rise of a Superstate

Leonid Brezhnev came to power in 1964 in a Soviet Union that was almost universally recognised as one of the two great superpowers of the modern world, although it was a claim challenged by Communist China. It was a remarkable position in which the USSR found itself, given that 50 years before, on the eve of World War I, the Russian empire had been regarded as one of the most economically backward of the then great powers. One perception had changed little: in 1964 the political and social systems of the USSR were seen as being totally at variance with the liberal tradition as represented by the 'Free World'; but in 1914 the Russian empire had also been regarded as being out of step both politically and socially with the parliamentary states of Western Europe and the USA. There were elements both of continuity and striking change in the Russian and Soviet experience.

Defeat during World War I had exacerbated Russia's problems and had led to a revolution in March 1917 which seemed to promise a liberal future for the country. But the Provisional Government proved no more capable than the Tsar of achieving military victory, and a small group of Marxist revolutionaries was able to exploit the power vacuum in the great cities and seize power in the November Revolution. The next few years were dominated by the efforts of Lenin and his associates to keep power in the face of hostile forces at home and abroad, whilst initiating radical economic, political and social changes, as befitted the world's first Socialist state.

By the end of the 1920s Joseph Stalin had assumed dictatorial powers in the USSR. Under his leadership, the country underwent a dramatic economic revolution at least as profound as the political revolution of 1917. The economic revolution comprised two strands: the collectivisation of agriculture, bringing the rural areas of the USSR securely under Soviet control; and a programme of centrally planned and centrally directed industrialisation designed to turn the USSR into a modern, powerful state, albeit under the close control of the Communist Party. Enormous social dislocation was the price paid by the Soviet people for these developments, but Stalin fulfilled many of his aims through a mixture of exhortation, appeals to national pride, massive propaganda drives, and a campaign of terror against real or imagined opponents. Millions of Soviet citizens were liquidated, or else languished in the camps of the *Gulag*, whilst the Party relentlessly extended its control over every aspect of Soviet life.

Stalin's USSR was almost destroyed by the German invasion of 1941, an invasion prompted by Hitler's ambition to subjugate Russia, destroy Communism, and create an empire in the East for the German 'master race'. Enormous damage was done to the USSR during the Great Patriotic War of 1941-45: thousands of villages and towns were destroyed, industries were demolished by the Germans or the Soviets themselves, and millions of Soviet soldiers and civilians were killed. However, the Soviets fought a total war from the start, inspired by appeals to their patriotism rather than by Communist zeal, and it was the heroic efforts of the Red Army, reinforced by a fully mobilised war economy, which, in Winston Churchill's phrase, 'tore the guts out of the German Army'.

2 Cold War Superpower

Despite the damage inflicted on the USSR during the war, it emerged in 1945 stronger than ever. The defeat of Germany left a power vacuum in Central Europe. Stalin had no powerful neighbour to fear. But to ensure that Soviet borders could not be threatened again, a 'buffer zone' was created throughout Eastern Europe: the victorious Red Army 'liberated' the countries of that region, and during the next few years Communist governments were installed, with Soviet help. The Eastern European states of Czechoslovakia, Hungary, East Germany, Poland, Romania and Bulgaria were soon further bound to the USSR by economic and military agreements.

These events brought the USSR into a new type of conflict with the USA and its Western allies. This was the Cold War, a state of tension between the Communist East and capitalist West that manifested itself in mutual recrimination and crises such as the Berlin Blockade of 1948-9 and the Korean War of 1950-53, but a situation in which the outbreak of a major war involving head-on confrontation between the two superpowers, possibly involving nuclear weapons, was avoided. The closely guarded frontier between Communist Eastern and democratic Western Europe, the so-called 'Iron Curtain', was a physical manifestation of the Cold War. Historians argued about the responsibility for the Cold War. One school interpreted it as arising from Soviet attempts to spread Communism by force, in keeping with the original Marxist tenet of world revolution. Proponents of this view maintained that such attempts by Stalin and his successors were only held in check by a vigilant West. Revisionist historians saw this as a simplistic interpretation, and emphasised legitimate Soviet security interests on Russia's frontiers, and apportioned some blame to the West for the Cold War tensions. Other historians have refused to apportion blame to either side, preferring instead to see the Cold War as something not arrived at by design, but a state of affairs that developed gradually and awkwardly as the two new superpowers adjusted to a new world: first sending conflicting signals to each other, and then learning to live with each other, albeit uncomfortably.

3 Khrushchev and De-Stalinisation

Stalin's power within the USSR was unchallenged whilst he was alive. However, three years after his death in 1953, his eventual successor, Khrushchev, condemned Stalin for his brutality, his arbitrariness and his mistakes, all of which he had inflicted on the Soviet people during 25 years of dictatorship. The denunciation came in Khrushchev's 'secret speech' to the Twentieth Party Congress. However, Khrushchev was himself part of the Soviet system, and had no intention of overturning it, only of modifying some of its more arbitrary aspects. There were attempts to introduce economic and administrative reforms, seen to be necessary now that the USSR had completed the first phase of economic revolution. But the essentials of the Soviet system - one-party control, the authoritarian state, central planning, pervasive influence over all aspects of peoples' lives as an effective means of social control - all remained in place. Nor was the USSR prepared significantly to relax its control over Eastern Europe, as the crushing of the Hungarian rising of 1956 demonstrated. The Soviet system did become less arbitrary, and ordinary citizens no longer lived in fear of sudden arrest by the secret police, but most controls were still in place. Even so, there was entrenched opposition from within the Party and the bureaucracy to Khrushchev's attempts to tinker with the economic and administrative structure. These involved, for example, a limited decentralisation of power in order to make the economy more responsive to real needs rather than those predetermined by the state. Such opposition from within the system would also frustrate later reformers.

Khrushchev further upset his colleagues by his populist and unconventional style of leadership, and his climb-down in response to American pressure during the Cuban Missile Crisis. Khrushchev was summarily sacked. At least the system had changed to the extent that he was allowed to live peaceably in retirement, and a change in leadership was no longer accompanied by widespread and bloody purges.

4 Brezhnev, 1964-82

Khrushchev's successor as Soviet leader was Leonid Brezhnev. He led the USSR until his death in 1982. After a cautious beginning, in which the virtues of collective leadership were emphasised, Brezhnev gradually amassed great personal power. He was allowed to do so mainly because he appeared to promise stability, a government by consensus, and an end to uncertainty. Certainly Soviet citizens had little to fear if they conformed, and standards of living for many of them did rise, although not to the extent that Khrushchev had promised some years before.

Caution could easily degenerate into inaction, and one of the criticisms made of Brezhnev's rule by later Russian historians was that he presided over a period of stagnation: much-needed economic and administrative reforms were neglected, and the underlying problems of an economy which was slowing down mounted. Party bureaucrats, secure in their jobs and privileges for life, saw no virtue in upsetting the apple cart. Brezhnev was no more inclined than Khrushchev to radically alter Soviet domestic or foreign policy. Open dissent against the system was punished by imprisonment in camps or mental institutions.Under Brezhnev the USSR expanded its influence world-wide by increasing its military forces, and strict control over Eastern Europe was maintained by the Brezhnev Doctrine. The crushing of the Czech reforming experience in 1968 echoed the treatment of Hungary in 1956. But Brezhnev also sought détente, or a relaxation of tension with the West. This was achieved, but it was not long lasting, and Soviet global ambitions placed great strain on the Soviet economy.

5 The Andropov-Chernenko Interregnum

Brezhnev's death in 1982 did not bring an end to the system. There followed an interregnum of three years under Andropov and Chernenko, years full of political manoeuvrings as the old and new political generations sought to maintain or extend their influence, and to implement their own ideas on how the USSR should develop.

Andropov was of an older generation, but he did recognise the need for domestic reform, and he promoted younger colleagues who saw eye-to-eye with him. Andropov's death saw the elevation of the unimpressive Chernenko, very much of the Brezhnev era, and sharing his old master's views on stability and the desirability of a cautious approach to government. However, Chernenko's tenure of office was widely interpreted at the time and since as being a stop-gap measure, whilst the ground was prepared for the more dynamic Gorbachev to assume the helm, which he did in 1985.

6 Gorbachev's USSR

Gorbachev was perceived in the West as a reformer. He certainly recognised the need for change in the USSR. However, he too started cautiously, with the intention of making the Soviet system work better. Even though, as part of *glasnost,* the Soviet people were invited to be more critical of their managers and administrators, and less tolerant of corruption, waste and inefficiency, Gorbachev's intention was to keep the Communist Party in control of the reforming process. However,

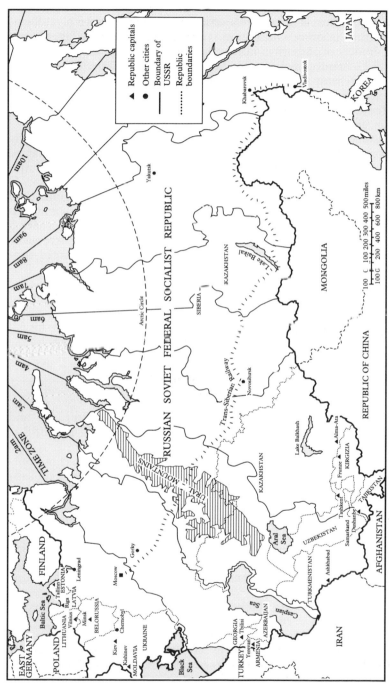

The USSR at the time of Brezhnev's coming to power

once people's expectations were raised, it became increasingly difficult to control the process of reform. Gorbachev discovered, like several other leaders of authoritarian societies, that the most dangerous period for those in control is often when the reins have been loosened. He faced opposition from conservatives who feared for their own privileged positions, or who were genuinely upset at the prospect of overturning all that they had been taught to hold dear; and also from those who became disillusioned as the reforms failed to deliver the goods.

Perestroika, or restructuring, did not solve the USSR's economic problems. Modifying or overturning political structures in order to encourage genuine popular participation also proved fraught with difficulties in a society without democratic roots.

Gorbachev achieved more on the world stage. He helped to initiate an ending to the Cold War and, of equal significance, he tolerated and even encouraged the break-up of Soviet control in Eastern Europe in such a way that instability was kept to a minimum. But these achievements carried little weight with Soviet citizens concerned about bread-and-butter issues at home.

Whether one man could have succeeded in reforming the Soviet political and economic system is doubtful. Gorbachev was certainly not capable of doing so. Although he survived an attempted coup, events had already overtaken Gorbachev's limited vision, and therefore his fall was inevitable. Gorbachev's fall was followed shortly afterwards by the collapse of the USSR itself.

7 Stalinism and Beyond, 1964-91

What were the features of the Soviet system that Brezhnev and Gorbachev inherited, and what were the problems faced by the USSR as it strove to maintain its position on the world stage?

In some of its fundamentals, the USSR had not changed radically since Stalin's day, and this was a major reason for the problems increasingly evident during the era of Brezhnev and Gorbachev, as they tried to maintain and extend Soviet influence as a great power in an increasingly complex world. This book will in part analyse how the last Soviet leaders coped with these problems.

In his book, *Stalinism* (Macmillan, 1990), Graeme Gill identified several features of what we call 'Stalinism'. This term was used to conveniently label the Soviet economic, political, social and cultural structures which developed during Stalin's lifetime, but in many respects also continued after 1953 - although Stalin himself never acknowledged the word as a description of his regime.

A key feature of Stalinism was a highly centralised economic system, directed from the centre, geared to targets, and with a strong emphasis on heavy industry. This was the means by which the USSR had hauled itself into the modern industrial age. It was an effective tool for industrialising an economy developing from a relatively primitive base, but was not suited to the more complex demands of a sophisticated society, and was unresponsive to the needs of consumers. This was recognised by Khrushchev, but his attempts to decentralise the economy were not much more than tinkering, and were frustrated anyway by bureaucratic obstruction. Brezhnev paid more attention to consumer demand, and planning adjustments did lead to a rise in the standard of living, but the essentials of the planned economy remained intact. Gorbachev was more frank in his recognition of the problems, and *perestroika* was an attempt to reverse the growing economic stagnation which was threatening to keep the USSR as a second-rate economy on the world stage. But even Gorbachev did not face up to all the implications of the transition from a highly centralised economy to a free-market one.

Gill also identified a Stalinist social structure which had once been fairly fluid: there had been an enormous demand for administrators and technicians, and tens of thousands of Soviet citizens from ordinary backgrounds, but with a smattering of education, had been able to rise to prominent positions in the new USSR, usually through the Party. However, once in power, they had mainly consolidated their privileges, which were passed on to their children. The prevailing ethos then became one of conservatism rather than revolutionary idealism. Brezhnev was a product of this system and accepted it, and the notion of privilege and 'jobs for life' became even more firmly entrenched, particularly as Stalinist purges became a thing of the past. Gorbachev was conscious of the detrimental effects of this process - after all, those who do well out of an existing political or social system are always likely to obstruct reform - but he never succeeded in radically reforming structures, or attitudes amongst the people who mattered, once he had accepted the need for changes.

Gill pointed out that, under Stalinism, cultural and intellectual life served the state, and that the State politicised all spheres of life and maintained the right to control them. This continued in the Brezhnev era: any attempt by intellectuals to criticise the system was not tolerated. Propaganda and indoctrination reinforced the system, although it was increasingly difficult to pretend, for example, that the Soviet people had a higher standard of material life than Western peoples when it was increasingly obvious to the Soviet people themselves from contact with the West that this was not the case.

Gorbachev's policy of *glasnost* was an attempt to allow ordinary people to think for themselves and to criticise. This was a difficult transition for a population brought up to accept only one official interpretation of what was good for themselves and the state, but, as Gorbachev emphasised, it was a necessary stage if restructuring were to work.

Gill also analysed a political system which was based upon personal dictatorship, reinforced by terror - the hallmark of the Stalinist era.

Some of the more arbitrary and brutal aspects had been relaxed under Khrushchev. Although Brezhnev held more titles than Stalin ever did, he was not as powerful, or as feared. Clearly he was the guiding force in the Soviet hierarchy, but his method of rule depended far more upon consensus than the exercise of arbitrary personal power, and the fate of Khrushchev was a reminder of what could happen to a general secretary who was too much out of step with the majority of his Party colleagues.

Gorbachev appeared to be in a strong personal position in the early years of his general secretaryship. But within five years he would be the most impotent leader the USSR had had, and by the time of his resignation he was in danger of becoming little more than a figurehead, as the changes which he had helped to initiate overtook him. Gorbachev's weakness was compounded by the fact that the arbitrary use of terror as a political weapon had effectively died with Stalin. Although Brezhnev's USSR remained authoritarian, and did not tolerate blatant challenges to its legitimacy, Gorbachev's USSR was increasingly a country in which the old rules and conventions of authority were crumbling: the Party and the instruments of power lost their monopolistic position as the leading forces in, and self-proclaimed protectors of, society.

Gill identified yet more features of Stalinism. One was a centralisation of authority paralleled paradoxically by a weakness of central control. In practice there was a good deal of independent initiative exercised outside Moscow: in some republics the local Party organisations operated virtually as independent fiefdoms. Gill also identified a conservative political ethos which developed out of original revolutionary enthusiasm, and which militated against change in favour of the status quo.

Both these features of Soviet life were still evident in the USSR of Brezhnev and Gorbachev. Brezhnev, along with most of the ruling élite and the Party bureaucracy, positively welcomed this conservative ethos: after all, it was an ethos which guaranteed their own security and privileges. Conversely, it was this ethos which frustrated Gorbachev and the reformers when they tried to initiate change.

The attributes of Stalinism outlined above are only one analysis of the USSR at the time of Stalin and after. There may be other legitimate interpretations. However, these examples are a useful tool in helping to explain those elements of continuity throughout the period 1964-91, and those elements which changed; and they help to explain some of the problems and issues which were to a large extent ignored, or swept under the carpet, by Brezhnev, and then were eventually tackled by Gorbachev, with mixed success. The extent to which these two regimes coped with governing the world's largest country, based upon an economic and political system which, in its essentials, developed two generations before in very different circumstances, is the principal theme of this book.

This theme can be summarised in the form of certain key questions:

a) To what extent would the political and economic system of Stalin and Khrushchev be retained, modified or overturned by their successors?

As has already been suggested, there were pressures from within the USSR both to retain the fundamentals of the Soviet system as established by Stalin, and only modified by Khrushchev, and to change it radically. The conservatives won the day under Brezhnev. To what extent did this serve the interests of the Soviet people? Were the future prospects of the regime damaged? Following Brezhnev's death there was a struggle for power. Gorbachev emerged as the victor. How sincere was his commitment to reform? How great were the obstacles to progress? How significant were the policies of *glasnost* and *perestroika*?

b) How would relations between the USSR and the rest of the world develop?

Under Stalin the regime had devoted most of its energies to national development rather than world revolution. By the time of Brezhnev, the USSR was firmly established as a superpower. Between 1964 and 1990 relations with the capitalist world went through periods of Cold War, crisis and détente. Relationships with the non-capitalist world also went through difficult periods. How successfully did the USSR sustain and develop a world role? Did the effort to do so play a significant part in the changes inside the USSR? What was the relationship between domestic and external policies? What was the Soviet contribution to the ending of the Cold War and the creation of a new world order?

c) Why did the Soviet Union break up?

In 1964 the control of the Communist Party over the Soviet republics seemed secure. Less than 30 years later the Union had dissolved, and the peoples of the former USSR faced an uncertain future. To what extent did the economic and political problems themselves lead to the break-up, or did the efforts of the reformers actually hasten the process? Was the break-up inevitable? What part did a rising tide of nationalism play? Was Gorbachev a victim of circumstances, or did he contribute to his own downfall?

An analysis of these fundamental issues will result in a better understanding of the complex events which unfolded as the USSR travelled through a period of stagnation and reform, from world power to decline.

Summary - 'The USSR under Brezhnev and Gorbachev - The Life and Death of a Superpower'

The following chronological table will be useful in giving you a framework for the whole period 1964-91 as you work through individual chapters and want a broad perspective, at the same time as studying detailed periods of time or events.

THE USSR, 1964-91

	Domestic Events	*Foreign Relations*
1964	Khrushchev sacked.	
	Brezhnev made first secretary.	
1966	Politburo reintroduced.	
1968		USSR and allies invaded Czechoslovakia.
1969		SALT talks in Helsinki.
1970		Treaties with Romania, Czechoslovakia and West Germany.
1971	Ninth Five-Year Plan ratified.	
1972	Visit of Nixon.	First SALT Treaty signed.
1973		Brezhnev visited USA and West Germany.
1974		Agreements on nuclear arms control.
1975	Helsinki Conference.	
1976	Tenth Five-Year Plan announced.	
1977	Brezhnev made head of state.	
	New constitution adopted.	
1978	Several prominent dissidents tried.	
1979		SALT II signed.
		USSR invaded Afghanistan.
1980	Death of Kosygin.	
1981	Next Five-Year Plan affirmed.	
1982	Death of Brezhnev.	
	Andropov elected general secretary.	
1983		South Korean aircraft shot down.
1984	Death of Andropov.	
	Chernenko elected general secretary.	
1985	Death of Chernenko.	
	Gorbachev elected general secretary.	
1986	Gorbachev proclaimed *perestroika* at Twenty-seventh Party Congress.	
	Calls for *glasnost*.	
	Chernobyl power station explosion	
1987	Supreme Soviet approved economic restructuring.	

1988   Outbreaks of nationalist violence.

Withdrawal of Soviet troops
from Afghanistan began.

1989   Cuts in military budget announced.

Gorbachev elected chairman of Supreme Soviet.

1990   Some republics declared their independence.

Warsaw Pact became a
political organisation.

Gorbachev appointed president.
Moves towards privatisation.

1991   Coup in Moscow. Break-up of Soviet Union.

Making notes on '*The USSR under Brezhnev and Gorbachev - The Life
and Death of a Superpower*'

At this stage, some of the ideas and even terms you have encountered
may make limited sense. They will become clearer as you work through
this book, particularly if you heed the advice on taking notes.

In making notes on this introductory chapter, the following headings,
subheadings and questions should assist you in understanding the
issues:

1   The rise of a superstate
1.1 Perceptions of the Soviet Union before 1964
1.2 How did the USSR develop economically and politically under
Stalin?
1.3 What effect did World War II have on the USSR?
2   Cold War superpower
2.1 The origins and nature of the Cold War. What were the arguments
about responsibility for the Cold War?
3   Khrushchev and de-Stalinisation
3.1 Khrushchev's de-Stalinisation. How effective was it?
4   Brezhnev, 1964-82
4.1 Brezhnev's method of government
4.2 Brezhnev's foreign policy
5   The Andropov-Chernenko interregnum
5.1 The policies of Andropov and Chernenko
6   Gorbachev's USSR
6.1 What were Gorbachev's motives for reform?
6.2 How successful was Gorbachev's foreign policy?
7   Stalinism and beyond, 1964-91
7.1 What was meant by 'Stalinism'?
7.2 The changing nature of the Soviet economy
7.3 The conservative social structure
7.4 Cultural controls
7.5 Personal dictatorship
7.6 Why did Gorbachev encounter major difficulties?

CHAPTER 2

The Years of Stagnation: Brezhnev's USSR, 1964-82

1 The Rise of Brezhnev

Leonid Brezhnev's rise to power was a lengthy affair, and typical of most leading Party figures among his contemporaries. Ambitious politicians had to work their way up through local, regional and Party positions, and even when they had powerful sponsors, their apprenticeship was frequently long. This was often a significant factor in Soviet government, for several reasons, not least of which was the fact that, having once reached the higher echelons of the Party, office holders were more likely to be set in their ways, enjoying the trappings of influence, and less likely to have reforming or interventionist tendencies. This was certainly true of Leonid Brezhnev.

Brezhnev came, like Khrushchev before him, from a humble background. He was born in 1906, the son of a steelworker. In 1923 Brezhnev joined the Komsomol, and in the late 1920s took part in the drive for collectivisation. He became a full Party member in 1931, and rose through the Party ranks, mainly due to the opportunities for promotion opened up by Stalin's purges and then the patronage of Khrushchev. When Khrushchev was given responsibility for purging the Party in the Ukraine, Brezhnev worked closely with him between 1938 and 1947. During World War II itself, Brezhnev was a political commissar with the Eighteenth Army. Thereafter he always maintained strong links with the armed services, as well as the Party, which he used to good effect. For example, he exploited his support within the military in helping to engineer Khrushchev's downfall. However, in the immediate post-war period, Khrushchev valued his capacity for administration, hard work and loyalty. Meanwhile, Brezhnev built up his own power base: he consolidated groups of loyal supporters in both the military and the administration. This 'Dnieper Mafia' was to play an important part in the rest of Brezhnev's career, as its members were promoted along with their patron.

In 1950 Brezhnev was put in charge of the Party machine in Moldavia. His task was to establish Soviet control in a sensitive area only recently acquired by the USSR from Romania. By successfully destroying opposition to Communist rule in Moldavia, liquidating its *kulaks* or rich peasants, and collectivising agriculture, Brezhnev came to the attention of Stalin himself. Stalin appointed him to the Central Committee and the Secretariat, and eventually the Politburo in 1952. In 1953 he was promoted within the Defence Ministry, with the military rank of lieutenant-general. Brezhnev's rise was temporarily halted by Stalin's death, and he lost his new positions, but Khrushchev put him in charge of his Virgin Lands programme, and he was reinstated in the Secretariat and Politburo in 1956. Although his career was temporarily checked again in 1960, he kept a high profile by means of meetings with foreign diplomats. Brezhnev was sensible enough to distance himself from Khrushchev as the latter came under increasing attack, and he soon began to attack Khrushchev's policies himself. Although Brezhnev had become Khrushchev's number two in 1960, little was known about him outside his immediate circle. He rose to the top not only because he was a skilled political operator, but because he was a man of the centre. Brezhnev represented the majority view, at least within the Party, on most issues. He was to be in power longer than any Soviet leader other than Stalin, and yet he moved into a position of dominance after Khrushchev in a low-key manner, because the ground had been well prepared. The Party leadership felt that it had little to fear from Brezhnev, and this was also the message transmitted outside the USSR.

Brezhnev's public image was very different from that of the effervescent Khrushchev. He was regarded as an unassuming, conscientious Party operator, who preferred not to take sides in disputes. Since he had served his political apprenticeship in the Stalin era, he was certainly not a political innocent, but Brezhnev's attraction to the Party apparatus was that he was regarded, rightly, as a conservative who would not promote radical ideas or act in an unpredictable fashion like Khrushchev. Therefore the key question was: would Brezhnev try to come to terms with a number of problems facing the USSR, or would he stick to the status quo and run the risk of economic and possibly social stagnation?

The requirements of Soviet propaganda meant that a personality cult of gross proportions was eventually built up around Brezhnev, and a long period in office seduced him into believing some of the propaganda. Brezhnev was conscious of his humble origins and wanted to be taken seriously as an intellectual, as well as a politician and an administrator. This yearning resulted in a series of ghosted books, such as *Little Land,* which purported to be an account of Brezhnev's glorious part in the campaign of 1943 on the Eastern Front, which in reality was very modest.

Privately, Brezhnev's life was much less grey than his public image. As leader, he used to spend time at Zavidovo, a wooded area near Moscow where Politburo members relaxed, hunted, and entertained foreign guests. Brezhnev had a fleet of Zil cars, which he liked to drive fast. He also used to listen to short-wave radio, and particularly to the 'Voice of America', which broadcast to Europe. Brezhnev enjoyed listening to its analysis of political developments inside the Kremlin, in which he himself was involved. Brezhnev also had his eccentricities. One was to arm-wrestle with colleagues, who usually ensured that they lost. Brezhnev beat the American President Nixon in such a contest when flying from Washington to California in 1973, and he made Gorbachev compete with him when the latter first entered the Politburo.

2 Consolidating Power

Soon after Khrushchev's fall, the Central Committee decided in October 1964 that no man should ever again be able to concentrate power in his own hands. Therefore it was agreed that the top posts in the Party and government should not be combined. It was to be a collective leadership. Brezhnev was appointed first secretary on 15 October 1964, and the following day Alexei Kosygin was made prime minister.

Kosygin was regarded in some foreign capitals as a relative lightweight compared to Brezhnev. But initially he was a very significant figure, who had served an impressive political apprenticeship: deputy prime minister at 36, prime minister of the Russian Federation at 39, and a member of the Politburo at 42. Although Kosygin was to disagree with Brezhnev over economic policy, they were not at odds personally. Kosygin attempted to reform the economy in 1965. Like many other Soviet reformers, he was to fail, and it was this failure which weakened him politically whilst Brezhnev's star waxed brightly.

Brezhnev had two priorities in 1964. One was to reassure his political and military colleagues that the unpredictability and instability of the Khrushchev years were at an end; and secondly, at a personal level, to ensure that his own political position was secure.

Brezhnev criticised Khrushchev for 'the unjustified transferring and replacing of personnel'. Therefore he made relatively few changes lower down in the administration, although he promoted his own supporters in the Politburo. By 1981, eight of the full Politburo members, excluding Brezhnev himself, were his protégés; and four of these were part of his 'Mafia', having been associated with him since the 1940s when he had been a secretary in the Dnepropetrovsk region. It was a time of political stability. When elderly politicians retired in the Brezhnev era, they were replaced by other elderly politicians: the average age of Politburo members increased from 58 in 1960 to 68 in 1978. There was no dynamism or longing for radical change in the leadership. Equally, there were no extensive purges. One of Brezhnev's friends was given the resurrected post of minister of Internal Affairs as a means of securing the support of the police and the judiciary. Yuri Andropov was made head of the KGB in 1967 and promoted to the Politburo - the first time since Beria that one man had been in both positions - not in an attempt to raise the profile of the KGB, but to ensure Party control over it, the more so since two of Andropov's deputies were Brezhnev's own supporters. The new minister of Defence in 1967 was Marshal Grechko, another Brezhnev man.

The policy of maintaining stability among Party personnel was known as the 'stability of cadres'. Stability was also assured by the *Nomenklatura* system. This was a lengthy list of reliable Party personnel, from whom names were selected when appointments to all key positions in the Party and state machines were necessary. Loyalty was further reinforced by the system of privileges available to Party members who attained a certain level: special, well-stocked shops, *dachas* or country residences, and private medical facilities. These privileges aroused increasing resentment among ordinary people, and were later attacked by Party reformers like Boris Yeltsin.

Brezhnev's methods were very effective: quietly removing possible rivals and ensuring that his own men controlled key institutions. There was no overt opposition, partly because Brezhnev had prepared the ground well, and partly because the Party was reassured by Brezhnev's conservative approach, particularly in domestic affairs. Nikolai Podgorny, head of state and a prominent figure in the events surrounding Khrushchev's fall, might have been a rival, but in December 1965 he was moved sideways, to the less prestigious presidency.

By the time that Brezhnev delivered a typically dull eight-hour speech to the Twenty-third Party Congress in 1966, he was already in a very powerful position. The fiction was maintained that it was a collective leadership, but Brezhnev was already acting as *the* leader. He was praised extensively in the media. Brezhnev's position was secure, and it was to remain so for almost 18 years. Only when it was clear that he was dying and thus irrevocably on the way out did

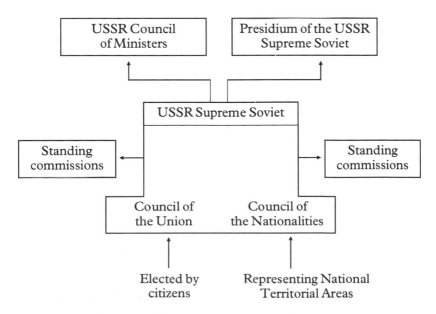

Supreme Soviet and government structure during the Brezhnev era

former colleagues begin to plot and intrigue behind his back.

It was significant that at the 1966 Congress, Brezhnev was already called general secretary rather than first secretary. The old Stalinist title had been resurrected. At the same time the Presidium was renamed the Politburo. Kosygin was an important political figure in his own right, but his reputation suffered from his failed attempt to reform the economy in 1965. He introduced some measures of decentralisation, which met such fierce opposition from the bureaucracy, still smarting from Khrushchev's reforming efforts, that they had to be abandoned. Kosygin was retired from public view in 1970.

As Kosygin's star waned, that of Brezhnev waxed. He combined leadership of the Party and state machines in 1970, as general secretary and president. He continued to increase his personal authority, not by personal charisma but by skilful consolidation of his power base, and by upholding the qualities of order, reassurance and consensus. These were qualities which still held great attractions for a generation that recalled the ruthlessness of the Stalin years and the unpredictability of the Khrushchev ones. Many Party secretaries and ministers appointed in 1964 were still in office at the time of Brezhnev's death in 1982.

Unsurprisingly, the Party showed signs of stagnation. Up to 1964, under Khrushchev there had been a period of sustained growth in Party membership. Afterwards there were stricter admission requirements, and the annual rate of growth in the Party declined from almost 7 per cent in 1965 to under 2 per cent by 1973. Thereafter the growth rate averaged about 2 per cent a year.

The fact that Brezhnev stood head and shoulders above his colleagues was emphasised by the fact that he did not have an obvious deputy or political heir marked out for the succession. At the Twenty-fifth Party Congress of 1976, Brezhnev was declared the 'universally acclaimed leader' of the Party, and he was created a marshal. In 1977 he removed Podgorny from the presidency and secured the consent of his colleagues to assume that role. A cult of personality was fostered, rivalling the excesses of Stalin's day. On his seventy-fourth birthday in December 1980, Brezhnev awarded himself the Second Order of the October Revolution. He already had four Orders of Lenin, a Victory Medal, the title of Hero of the Soviet Union, and the Lenin Peace Prize. Films were made about his life, and his modest wartime record was exaggerated to absurd lengths. There was much private cynicism and incredulity when Brezhnev was awarded the Lenin Prize for his memoirs, which were actually written by an aide. More cities and factories were named after him.

In 1981, at the Twenty-sixth Party Congress, Brezhnev was hailed as an 'outstanding political leader and statesman', the 'true continuer of Lenin's great cause' and an 'ardent fighter for peace and communism'. On his seventy-fifth birthday, in December 1981, he awarded himself more medals. Brezhnev actually had more medals than Stalin and

Khrushchev combined, and more military decorations than Marshal Zhukov, hero of Leningrad and Stalingrad, and captor of Berlin during World War II.

Shortly before Brezhnev's death, the entire Politburo and Secretariat were re-elected without any change, an unprecedented event. Both his son and son-in-law gained high positions in state and Party, and other members of his family, as well as colleagues, climbed on to the gravy train. Some became involved in shady practices and outright corruption.

3 'Developed Socialism'

Brezhnev enjoyed the widespread support of political colleagues whose privileges he promised to maintain, and from the majority of the population, which was promised a gradual improvement in its standard of living. The reaction to Kosygin's economic reforms of 1965 showed the difficulties of trying to change the existing order. But in 1971 Brezhnev was confident enough to declare the idea of 'Developed Socialism'. There were difficult ideological matters to be addressed. In 1961 Khrushchev had announced that the old Marxist concept of the 'Dictatorship of the Proletariat', supposedly exercised through the Party, had been overtaken by 'the state of the whole people'. In other words, Khrushchev was calling for mass participation in politics and society, on the grounds that everyone, not just a privileged élite, should be engaged in the business of creating Communism. This radical approach was combined with Khrushchev's Utopian declaration in his new Party programme that, having entered 'the period of full-scale construction of Communism', Socialism would give way to the fully-fledged classless Communist state of plenty by 1980. Khrushchev had also enunciated the doctrine of 'differing roads to Socialism': in other words, it might be possible to progress to the desired goal by means of a range of political systems, including parliamentary representation. This was effectively a recognition of reality: there were already divisions in the Socialist camp, with Yugoslavia and China following their own paths to Socialism, very different to the Soviet one. However, it seemed a dangerous doctrine for those Communist Party stalwarts who had long assumed that they represented a confident, monolithic, political-belief system that would inherit the future.

Brezhnev felt constrained to address these issues. But he had no intention of upsetting powerful groups with an ambitious reform programme, and it is significant that Stalin's reputation was partly rehabilitated at the Twenty-third Party Congress in 1966. In 1967 Stalinism was defined as a period of considerable achievement, marred only by 'unfortunate and temporary errors', a gross euphemism for Stalin's reign of terror. However, Brezhnev did at least emphasise that there could not be a return to the Stalinist past.

Brezhnev outlined his theory of 'Developed Socialism' in 1977:

1 The experience of the USSR, of other countries of the Socialist
community testifies to the fact that laying the foundations of
Socialism, that is, abolishing the exploiting classes and establishing
public ownershhip of the means of production in all sectors of the
5 national economy, does not yet make it possible to launch the
direct transition to Communism ...

It is self-evident that a mature Socialist society must rest on
highly developed productive forces, on a powerful, advanced
industry, on a large-scale, highly mechanised agriculture built on
10 collectivist principles. Such today is the Soviet economy ...

Thanks to the convergence of the diverse forms of Socialist
property, the gradual obliteration of any essential distinctions
between town and country, between mental and physical labour,
and adoption by all working people of the ideological and political
15 positions of the working class, the interests and goals, the social
ideals and psychology of all strata of the population have drawn
closer together than ever before. On this basis substantial changes
have also occurred in the political system. Essentially in the
growing of the state of the dictatorship of the proletariat into a
20 Socialist state of all the people ...

... developed Socialism has now been built in the USSR, that is
to say, a degree, a stage in the maturing of the new society has been
reached when the repatterning of the totality of social relations on
the collectivist principles intrinsically inherent in Socialism is
25 completed.

Brezhnev accepted that, in the modern world, the Party did not have the
expertise to transform the USSR by its efforts alone - it was no longer the
vanguard. He was confident enough to predict that the same startling
technological and scientific achievements that were transforming many
capitalist economies would do the same for the USSR. However,
increasing evidence of economic problems in the Soviet Union in the
mid-1970s alarmed those in the Party who recognised the impossibility
of meeting the raised expectations of the ordinary people. So
'Developed Socialism' was quietly relegated to the backburner, as had
Khrushchev's optimistic pronouncements some years before. When it
became impossible for even the Soviet propaganda machine to disguise
the fact that living standards in the capitalist West were considerably
higher than those in the USSR, it attacked the evils of 'consumerism' -
associated with greed, 'parasitism', and a range of social problems
suffered in capitalist society. Soviet propaganda painted a stark contrast,
eulogising the 'qualitative superiority' of life in a Socialist state like the
USSR over capitalism.

Structure of the Communist Party of the Soviet Union

Representative bodies		Executive bodies	Administrative bodies
Party Congress	Central Committee	Politburo	Secretariat
↑	↑	↑	↑
Republican Party Congress	Republican Central Committee	Republican Party Bureau	Republican Secretariat
↑		↑	↑
Regional Party Conference	Regional Committee	Regional Bureau	Regional Secretariat
↑	↑	↑	↑
District Party organisation	District Committee	District Bureau	District Secretariat
↑			↑
Local Party organisation			Secretary

A note on the structure of the Communist Party and the Soviet Union

The Council of the Union (elected by the people) and the Council of Nationalities (elected by the republics and territorial areas) together made up the Supreme Soviet, or parliament, of the USSR. The Supreme Soviet met at least twice a year, and the deputies were part-time citizens supposedly representing different sections of the population. Although the Supreme Soviet did consider legislation put before it, it was an opportunity for the government to explain its policies rather than for genuinely democratic decisions to be made. The Standing Commissions, elected by the deputies, were more important in initiating legislation, supervising ministries, and commenting upon economic plans. The Supreme Soviet also elected the Council of Ministers, or government, of the USSR. The smaller Presidium was a standing body which dealt with the day-to-day business of government.

This structure worked in parallel with Party organisations. The Party retained the crucial right to determine the main aims of national policy in all major areas.

The local Party branches usually met once a month, to monitor the activities of ordinary Party members and to consider local Party business. Above these local Party cells were a series of Party organisations up to Republican level and finally, Union level. At each level congresses were held, and these elected committees to supervise Party affairs between congresses; they in turn elected bureaux and secretariats which comprised full-time Party administrators. Although all Party posts were elective, once elected, lower bodies were required to obey the decisions made by the individual or organisation on the next step in the structure.

The national Party Congress met every five years, and not only discussed Party affairs but, crucially important, elected the Central Committee, which was responsible for the Party between congresses. The Central Committee elected both the Politburo, the body which met weekly to make policy, and the Secretariat, which ran the Party organisation and carried out the Politburo's decisions. The general secretary was also elected by the Central Committee, and he chaired meetings of both the Politburo and the Secretariat.

'My loving care and attention will help me farm!' 1971 poster

'Our hopes and deeds belong to Mother Russia and the Party!' 1976 poster

4 Economic Stagnation

Economic problems could not, however, be explained away completely. The problems were not new. There had been a dramatic industrial upturn under Stalin, because the Soviet economy had progressed from a low economic base in the 1920s, and so the blunt instrument of the Five-Year plans had produced impressive results in terms of quantity. But the methods of the command economy were far less effective as a means of meeting the needs of a more sophisticated economy, in which quality rather than sheer quantity was vital. The Soviet economy was already slowing down in the 1950s, in terms of both growth and of worker productivity.

Ironically, one of the most successful sectors of the Soviet economy was the 'unofficial' part, or the black economy. It accounted for up to 25 per cent of the gross national product by the time of Brezhnev's death. In order to avoid queueing and shortages, it was necessary to bribe and to barter for goods. An atmosphere of corruption and nepotism therefore flourished.

Khrushchev had recognised the reality, but he did not have the support to initiate major structural changes to the economy, and the reforms which he did attempt would not have radically improved the situation. The underlying trend of economic slowdown continued. The conscious Soviet effort to compete industrially and militarily with the USA on a global basis, following the Soviet humiliation over Cuba, simply worsened things and caused bigger strains. More and more resources were devoted to defence products - not just money, but expertise too. Even before the Cuban crisis, in 1962, Soviet national income had been about half that of the USA, whilst consumption per head had been only about a quarter.

The situation became so serious that discussions about reform, however unwelcome, had to begin. In September 1962 *Pravda* had, presumably with official approval, already published the reforming ideas of Liberman, an economics professor from Kharkov. In outline, these ideas were a model for the Gorbachev reforms 20 years later: whilst retaining a belief in planning, Liberman's argument was that the central planning agency should concentrate on long-term strategic planning, whilst managers should be given more power to make decisions at the local level. Even more controversially, 'profitability' was suggested as the criterion by which performance should be assessed, rather than the capacity to meet demand or the regime's perceived needs. This smacked dangerously of market economics so, unsurprisingly, the proposals were vague. Even so, they provoked an outcry from conservatives.

Partly in response to this criticism, a comprehensive reform programme was outlined in a series of articles written by an academic, Vasili Nemchinov, between 1962 and 1964. Nemchinov saw economic reform as a means of strengthening state control of the economy.

Although not arguing for a democratisation of society as a whole, he did insist that economic progress depended upon the 'creativity of the popular masses' and more independence for management. A generation on, Gorbachev was to cite Nemchinov as the inspiration for *perestroika*. Nemchinov's views were to be the basis of Gorbachev's 1987 reform measures, which failed, and in failing Gorbachev was persuaded that it was impossible to achieve radical economic reform without a corresponding democratisation of the political system.

During the Brezhnev years there were clear limits to what could be seriously discussed. For example, whatever the merits of encouraging self-management on economic grounds, it was politically unacceptable to go beyond a certain point. Self-management would have reduced Party control in rural areas - and Party control had been precisely one of the reasons *why* Stalin had introduced collectivisation in the late 1920s.

Discussions on economic reform continued in a low key throughout the 1970s, but without any reference to possible accompanying political reform. Price reform was considered: the existing system of subsidising basic prices was very expensive and inefficient. But the regime did not wish to face the social consequences of price rises. One historian wrote: 'Preserving the existing irrational structure of prices while increasing enterprise autonomy was one of the factors lying behind the deterioration of the Soviet economy in 1988-9'. Conservatives used events such as the Czechoslovakian crisis of 1968, which followed attempts to introduce radical changes into a Communist state, to highlight the dangers of reform.

In Brezhnev's USSR there was virtually no link between academic economists and Party operatives. However, elements of both groups continued to propose some modifications to the planning system in the late 1970s and early 1980s. Already in 1972 the regime had accepted the concept of a 15-year programme with scientific and technical goals, linked to economic progress, but the concept died a death because *Gosplan* would not tolerate a rival planning agency. There was recognition that one- and five-year plans were not necessarily the most rational system of planning, and thus the talk was instead of 15- or 20-year plans. There were occasional positive references too to economic reforms in Hungary, and these influenced Andropov. Soon after Brezhnev's death, an economist was to be promoted to the Politburo for the first time in many years - Vadim Medvedev, who published a book in 1983 arguing for more flexibility, and this was another influence on the Gorbachev reforms. But progress was slow. Thinkers were constrained by the official ideology, which regarded market-orientated systems as heresy. Nobody really got to grips with the fact that the Soviet economy was slowing down. When it became too difficult to disguise the reality of economic stagnation, the Central Statistical Administration simply cut down on the amount of published statistics!

Brezhnev's government copied some organisational features of the

American economy: between 1973 and the end of the decade over half the Soviet factories and enterprises were consolidated into production associations on the lines of US-owned multinationals. Before that, Khrushchev's Supreme Council of the National Economy was abolished, and in 1965 Kosygin introduced some reforms which anticipated those of Gorbachev: industrial enterprises were given some autonomy, wages were linked to output, and prices to demand. Kosygin had encountered entrenched opposition from bureaucrats brought up on the gospel of centralised planning, and from managers who were unused to taking risky decisions, preferring instead to rely upon orders from above.

In the late 1970s Brezhnev turned his attention to agriculture. He drew upon his own experience in Moldavia to develop 'agro-industrial complexes'. This meant situating light industries such as food-processing factories close to the fields, while collective and state farms were organised into yet larger units. This policy was aimed not just at increasing agricultural production, which was certainly necessary, but also at equalising living standards between town and country. Since Stalin's industrialisation drive, living standards had been lower in rural areas, and they were to remain so even after Brezhnev's reforms. Restrictions on peasants' private plots were eased; by 1981 peasants finally acquired the right to internal passports, and farmers gained minimum incomes and the same pension rights as industrial workers. One-quarter of all meat and dairy produce came from private plots, reflecting the effort which peasants put into the care of these relatively small areas of land.

Investment in agriculture increased, and the policy of amalgamating collective farms and converting some into state farms continued, but there was no lasting increase in production. Between 1968 and 1977 3.5 million tractors, 1 million combine harvesters and 2 million lorries were supplied to the agricultural sector. By 1980 there were 26,000 collective farms and 21,000 state farms in the USSR. The responsibility for agriculture after 1978 was given to Gorbachev.

	Produced national income	Gross industrial production	Gross agricultural production	Labour productivity	Real incomes per head
1961-5	6.5	8.6	2.3	6.1	3.6
1966-70	7.8	8.5	3.9	6.8	5.9
1971-5	5.7	7.4	2.5	4.5	4.4
1976-80	4.3	4.4	1.7	3.3	3.4
1981-5	3.6	3.7	1.1	3.1	2.1

Annual average rates of growth (%) of the Soviet economy during the Brezhnev era

The results of this investment were disappointing. Agricultural yields remained one-third of those in Western Europe, and agricultural productivity was one-quarter of that in the USA. Investment in agriculture increased to 27 per cent by 1977, and during this period the USSR probably subsidised agriculture more than any other country in the world. Agriculture employed 22 per cent of the workforce, and yet it contributed only 17 per cent of the national income. In 1975 the USSR had to sign a five-year agreement with the USA to buy a minimum of 6 to 8 million tons of grain per year.

Soviet economic performance was particularly disappointing since the signs for industrial and technological advance should have been promising. Siberia began to rise to economic prominence in the 1970s, following the discovery of oil in western Siberia in 1964 and the uncovering of massive mineral resources. By 1983 357 million tons of oil were being exploited in Siberia, representing over 60 per cent of the annual Soviet oil production. The development of vast, newly discovered reserves of gas and coal was given a high priority in the Tenth and Eleventh Five-Year plans of 1976-80 and 1981-5. Between 1974 and 1984 30 billion roubles were spent on the 3,145 kilometres of the Baikal-Amur (BAM) Railway, designed to exploit this natural wealth. Billions of roubles were also spent on the 3,500-mile-long Siberian gas pipeline.

Nor were other areas neglected. There was some investment in southern and Asian regions such as Turkestan. However, some projects were disastrous: for example, irrigation schemes in Kazakhstan involved the diversion of rivers, and this led to the drying-up of the Aral Sea, with serious ecological consequences.

What scientific progress there was, was largely confined to the prestigious defence and space industries rather than the civilian economy. Sectors which were rapidly developing in the West, such as computer technology, were neglected, partly because access to basic typewriters and Xerox machines, let alone personal computers, was regarded as being a security risk.

Industrial growth not only slackened but declined sharply. The targets set by the Ninth Five-Year Plan of 1971-5 were not met by either agricultural or industrial output. Consumer-goods production was planned to overtake capital-goods production during the period of this plan, but it did not happen. Targets were not met for several reasons: pressure from the defence and other powerful sectors which prevented the diversion of resources; an inefficient and unproductive workforce operating at half the efficiency of its American counterpart; shortages of labour; costlier fuel and transport - all contributed to the failures. The regime was aware of the problem, and both the Tenth and Eleventh Plans of 1976-80 and 1981-5 reduced the emphasis on increasing productive capacity in favour of more efficiency and quality. However, although more consumer goods did come onto the market, poor quality remained a problem, and the decline in the growth of gross national product continued. The rate of economic growth was at its lowest in the early 1980s.

The fundamentals of the system remained in place, and there would be no further attempt at substantial economic reform until the Gorbachev era. Indeed, the Kosygin reforms probably had a detrimental effect: by promising higher incomes, stability and security for managers and the workforce, and stable, subsidised prices for the consumer, production costs went up, without the accompanying changes which might have guaranteed a corresponding increase in output. In certain respects the economic system became even more irrational: although managers could make more decisions, ministers continued to interfere in enterprises. The regime would not reach the obvious conclusion that a fundamental restructuring of ideas, strategy and organisation was necessary. Instead there was tinkering with the system and the odd change made here and there. This was particularly the case as Brezhnev grew older and the administrators, waiting for him to die, were reluctant to make long-term decisions.

5 Living and Working Conditions

The standard of living of many Soviet citizens did improve gradually under Brezhnev. One clear sign was the fact that by the mid-1980s only 15-18 per cent of the urban population lived in shared or communal apartments, compared to a figure of 40 per cent 20 years earlier. In contrast, investment in health spending declined from 6.5 per cent of the state budget to 5 per cent in 1980, whereas spending on defence remained high. In 1967 the five-day week became the norm, and holidays were increased from 12 to 15 working days a year. The minimum wage was increased, and real wages increased by almost 50 per cent between 1965 and 1977. Three times more young people were entering higher education by the end of Brezhnev's life, and the consumption of meat, fish and vegetables increased by 50 per cent. However, much of the increased output of consumer durable goods was of poor quality.

The majority of the Soviet population appeared satisfied with the existing level of job security, social services and educational provision. Even those Soviet citizens who emigrated expressed satisfaction with these aspects of their previous lives - it was the rigidity of the system, the discouragement of initiative, the stifling propaganda, and the limits on cultural, religious and intellectual freedom which irked many.

Although the personal incomes of Soviet citizens continued to grow, the disparities between different regions of the USSR also widened. The highest growth rates were in Belorussia and Moldavia, the lowest in Azerbaijan, Turkmenistan, Uzbekistan, Kirgizia and Tadzhikistan. In Estonia, collective-farm workers earned double the average for the

USSR as a whole.

There were extensive social problems in the Brezhnev era. Alcohol consumption, a drop in life expectancy, a rise in infant mortality, higher divorce rates, more single-parent families, an ageing population - all added to the regime's concerns, although their seriousness was rarely publically acknowledged. Over half the Soviet population was female, yet the role of women had scarcely improved since Stalin's day. Women were expected to have jobs as well as look after homes. Jobs in which they were heavily represented tended to be amongst the lower paid. Equality was a slogan, not the reality.

6 The Brezhnev Constitution

In addition to promoting and demoting colleagues, Brezhnev felt the need to make his mark politically in a more lasting and public way. A new constitution was introduced in 1977 to commemorate the sixtieth anniversary of the Revolution; it replaced the 1936 Stalin Constitution. The USSR was declared to be a Socialist state, one in which the 'dictatorship of the proletariat' had been achieved. The Communist Party was 'the leading and guiding force in Soviet society and the nucleus of the political system, of all state and public organisations'. The Communist Party 'exists for the people and serves the people ... The Communist Party, armed with Marxism-Leninism, determines the general perspectives of the development of society and the line of domestic and foreign policy of the USSR'. This was the famous Article 6, not repealed until after 1990.

The constitution contained guarantees of freedoms of speech, assembly, press and conscience, with the proviso that the rights of individual citizens 'must not injure the interests of society and the state and the rights of other citizens'. In reality, this promise meant little, because only the state could determine what the interests of society were. But Brezhnev trumpeted the constitution as being a guarantor of democracy:

1 Democracy, which is natural and necessary in the conditions of
  Socialism, is not something that is fixed and static in its forms,
  functions and manifestations. It develops as society develops as a
  whole. It is possible, of course, to assess the level of development of
5 Socialist democracy only if one has a clear criterion for doing so.
  Marxist-Leninists have such a criterion. Under Socialism, Lenin
  observed, 'for the first time in the history of civilised society, the
  mass of the population will rise to take an *independent* part, not only
  in voting and elections, *but also in the everyday administration of the*
10 *state*'. This was, and remains for us, the main criterion, the
  criterion which we take for measuring the success of our

democracy, determining the paths of its further development and improvement.
Leonid Brezhnev in *World Marxist Review*, December 1977.

7 Dissidence and Social Control

Under Brezhnev there were few signs of the regime relaxing its hold over the Soviet people. Rather, the powers of the police were strengthened; capital punishment was reintroduced for several offences, and the legal code was generally made tougher. It was persistently emphasised that the interests of the state were more important than those of the individual. Before Brezhnev, there had been an attempt to achieve more popular participation in the administration of justice: 'comrades' courts' and 'people's courts' had been encouraged to try cases according to a principle called 'Socialist legality', which supposedly guaranteed the rights of citizens. This notion was now reversed. It was assumed by the authorities that criticism of the Soviet system must be, if not attributable to outright treachery, a sign of psychological disturbance on the part of the individual.

The Brezhnev years were marked by a campaign against dissidents. The writers Sinyavsky and Daniel were the first to suffer, in 1965. The crushing of the Czech reform movement in 1968 also hardened attitudes towards dissent. Although some intellectuals, notably those associated with the journal *Novy Mir,* edited by Tvardovsky, argued for a more open approach to the arts, and there was a brief period of relaxation in the early 1970s, a further government crackdown followed. Some notable writers were expelled from the Union of Writers and emigrated: they included Josef Brodsky in 1972, Andrei Sinyavsky in 1973, and Alexander Solzhenitsyn in 1974. 'Unofficial' literature, the so-called *samizdat,* continued to circulate furtively in the USSR, despite the vigilance of the authorities.

In other areas the official attitude was somewhat more ambivalent. In the field of art, old Stalinist notions of Socialist realism still held sway officially, but it was possible for artists sometimes to exhibit avant-garde works. On the other hand, such exhibitions were sometimes broken up by the KGB. Similar developments took place in the field of music.

Dissent became an increasingly prominent issue in the Brezhnev era, although its significance was sometimes exaggerated outside the USSR. The human-rights movement which emerged in the late 1960s did receive a boost from the move towards détente in 1972. The Soviet government's endorsement of the Helsinki Accord in August 1975 created more interest. Several 'Helsinki groups' were formed to monitor Soviet observance of the agreement. However, although the groups were technically within the law, several of their prominent members were harassed, including the scientist and Nobel prizewinner Dr Andrei

Sakharov, the scientist Yuri Orlov, and the writer Andrei Ginzberg. From 1977 the KGB's attitude towards dissident groups became even more severe. Orlov was sentenced to seven years in a labour camp for 'anti-Soviet activities', followed by five years' internal exile. By 1978 over 20 members of the Helsinki groups were in prison. Sakharov was placed under house arrest in Gorki in 1980. Further arrests followed, and in September 1982 the Helsinki monitoring group was disbanded, with 60 of its 80 members having been tried or jailed, and most of the rest having been deported or having emigrated.

  Dissent was sometimes associated with religion or nationalist unrest. Soviet Jews increasingly demanded the right to emigrate, for religious reasons, or out of a desire for material betterment. During the 1970s 250,000 Jews left the USSR, the peak year being 1979, with 51,000 emigrants. By 1982 the numbers were being restricted: only 2,699 were allowed to leave in that year. The government's attitude towards Jewish emigration varied according to the progress or lack of progress in its relations with the West.

  Nationalist feeling in the Baltic republics was given an impetus by the growth of Catholic and trade-union activity in Poland. Helsinki monitoring groups were established in Catholic Lithuania; and nationalist demonstrations against 'Russification' broke out in Estonia and Latvia. Unofficial trade unions were active in the Ukraine, along with Catholic and fundamentalist Baptist groups. Occasional displays of nationalist discontent took place in Georgia and the Muslim republics. The Soviet regime acted particularly harshly against these sporadic outbreaks in Muslim areas, fearing the spread of Muslim fundamentalism into the USSR from bordering regions in the south. Within Russia itself there was a growth of Russian nationalist dissent, which became more prominent after Brezhnev.

  Although such expressions of dissent aroused much interest abroad, dissidents achieved little within the USSR itself. The regime, with its monopoly of channels of information, generally succeeded in portraying dissidents as belonging to privileged, ungrateful or unpatriotic factions, divorced from the everyday concerns of Soviet citizens.

  Many Soviet citizens were contemptuous of the dissidents' stand. An official view was put across in 1966:

1 The enemies of Communism are not squeamish. With what gusto do they dish up any 'sensation' gleaned from the garbage heap of anti-Sovietism! ... in brief, the enemies of Communism found what they were looking for - two renegades, for whom duplicity and
5 shamelessness had become a credo.
  ... They find nothing pleasing in our country, nothing in its multinational culture is sacred to them; they are ready to vilify and defame everything that is dear to Soviet man, whether it belongs to the present or the past ...

10   Sinyavsky and Daniel grew up in the Soviet Union. They
enjoyed all the blessings of Socialism. Everything that had been
won by our elder brothers and fathers in the flaming years of the
Revolution and the Civil War, and in the difficult period of the first
15   Five-Year plans was at their service.
Sinyavsky and Daniel began in a small way: they replaced
honesty with unprincipledness, literary activity as understood by
Soviet people with double-dealing, sincerity in their attitude to life
with nihilism and with carping criticism of their fellow men behind
20   their backs ... From petty meanness to major betrayal - such was
the route down which they marched ...
These are not merely moral monsters but active henchmen of
those who stoke the furnace of international tension, who wish to
turn the Cold War into a hot one, who have not abandoned the
25   mad dream of raising their hand against the Soviet Union ...
Essentially, these are shots fired in the back of a people fighting
for peace on earth and for universal happiness ...
Time will pass, and no one will even remember them. The pages
steeped in bile will rot in the dump. After all, history has time and
30   time again confirmed that slander, however thick and venomous it
be, inevitable evaporates under the warm breath of truth.

Yeremin, 'Turncoats', in *Izvestia*, 13 January 1966.

8 Stagnation

Events and policies drifted under Brezhnev. This was particularly
evident in Moscow's dealings with the outlying republics. Khrushchev,
by introducing more political and economic decentralisation, had
inadvertently strengthened the power of local élites or 'mafias' in some
republics. In Transcaucasia and Central Asia in particular, corruption
amongst Party officials was rife, and went unchecked as long as
republican leaders satisfied Moscow by restraining nationalist discontent. This state of affairs continued throughout Brezhnev's period in
office. Only in Transcaucasia, where the economy was suffering badly
from mismanagement and corruption, were outsiders brought in on any
large scale to rectify abuses. Shevardnadze was made head of the
Georgian Party in 1972, to root out corruption.

Brezhnev was anxious to avert any crisis. A Soviet joke circulated to
the effect that when he took power, he was handed three envelopes by
Khrushchev and told to open one when a crisis materialised. When he
opened one, a note inside read, 'Blame me for everything, and carry on'.
When the second crisis arrived, Brezhnev opened the second envelope:
the note inside read, 'Reshuffle the Politburo and carry on'. When the
third and final crisis came, and Brezhnev was desperate to find a
solution, he opened the third envelope. The contents read, 'Start writing

three envelopes'.

As Brezhnev's health declined in the late 1970s, so his dominance began to falter. The Politburo began to shrink as the old guard died off: Kosygin in 1980 and Suslov in 1982. Brezhnev himself was increasingly absent from the centre of affairs in Moscow, having never fully recovered from serious strokes in 1975 and 1977. Decision-making was increasingly delegated to other Politburo members, and to Brezhnev's private office, run by Chernenko, who was being groomed for the succession. But a struggle for power was going on behind the scenes long before Brezhnev's death in November 1982, and it was to be important in determining both the short- and the long-term future of the USSR.

Making notes on *'The Years of Stagnation: Brezhnev's USSR, 1964-82'*

When reading this chapter, you should think about the following issues:
(i) How did Brezhnev achieve dominance in the USSR, and what was his method of rule?
(ii) What economic problems were evident during the 1960s and 1970s, and how did the regime deal with them?
(iii) Did the condition of the Soviet people during this period improve? and
(iv) What legacy did Brezhnev leave the USSR?

The following headings and subheadings should provide a framework for your notes.
1   The rise of Brezhnev
1.1 Brezhnev's rise under Stalin and Khrushchev
1.2 Brezhnev's qualities and personality
2   Consolidating power
2.1 Changes in the administration
2.2 Brezhnev's leadership style
2.3 Personality cult
3   'Developed Socialism'
3.1 What was 'Developed Socialism'?
4   Economic stagnation
4.1 Discussion about economic reform
4.2 Obstacles to reform
4.3 Agricultural developments
4.4 Results of reforms
5   Living and working conditions
5.1 Changes in living and working conditions
6   The Brezhnev Constitution
6.1 The significance of the constitution
7   Dissidence and social control
7.1 Policy towards dissidents
7.2 Religious dissent
7.3 Nationalist dissent
8   Stagnation

Answering essay questions on 'The Years of Stagnation: Brezhnev's USSR, 1964-82'

The following are typical of the type of question which might be expected on the whole of this period of Brezhnev's rule in the USSR.

1   To what extent is the comment 'a period of authoritarianism and stagnation' an apt description of the USSR under Brezhnev?
2   How successfully did the Communist Party manage Soviet domestic affairs during the Brezhnev era (1964-82)?

These questions have similarities. Both cover a broad span of about 20 years, and also require some understanding of context: it would be difficult to answer either question fully without some knowledge of the internal situation of the USSR - politically, economically and socially - at the time of Khrushchev's fall from power in 1964. The questions also require you not only to consider the evidence, but to use it in order to arrive at a judgment.

When examiners set essays like this for examinations, they often have certain key themes in mind. When attempting any essay, in examination conditions or not, it is a good idea to go through certain stages of planning: a) identify the key words in the question; b) decide on the main theme of your essay; c) plan your essay - that usually means an introduction, a main body, and a conclusion.

The main body of your essay should be analytical: that is, you should ensure that you do not just write a narrative or a description of what happened during a particular period, but address the actual question, assertion or argument in the title. You will obviously mention events, facts, people and so on, but this information should be used to support your arguments. Do not include this information for its own sake, particularly if you are restricted by the constraints of time. Think of several key points you will make, and then develop them with supporting evidence in the main body of your essay.

Your conclusion should briefly summarise or synthesise (bring together) your main arguments - it should not be an opportunity to introduce new ideas or new material. Both these questions are 'To what extent ... ?' types: in other words, they ask for a judgment. If you can arrive at a clear judgment, do so; on the other hand, if you feel that the evidence is such that it is genuinely impossible to come down firmly on one side of the argument or another, that is equally valid. The important thing in either case is to support your views with evidence - which can only come from having studied and researched the topic. Reasonably wide reading is recommended.

The key phrases in question 1 are 'To what extent' and a 'period of authoritarianism and stagnation'. In deciding your theme, you should examine the meaning of the second phrase, and take each word in turn.

'Authoritarianism' implies a dictatorship or firm rule. Under this heading you should consider the activities of Brezhnev and the role of the Communist Party generally, and the means used to enforce authoritarian rule, such as the reliance on a one-party state, censorship, propaganda, and the role of the internal security forces. 'Stagnation' should be taken to include many different aspects - political, economic, social and intellectual. Therefore define your terms of reference very clearly.

When you have decided upon your headings, consider the evidence for each of them. A good answer is likely to show a broad perspective: for example, by comparing Brezhnev's regime with the previous and later ones, if you have that knowledge. You should then be able to make some sort of valid judgment and, provided that your argument is reasoned, you will get credit.

The key words in the second essay are 'How successfully' and 'the Communist Party'. Clearly, to answer this question you have to consider the function and activities of the Communist Party in the Soviet system, and during this period in particular. You might consider the different aspects of this influence: political, social, cultural and so on. Did the Party's role or personnel change significantly during this period? It is not just a question of considering the role of a few key individuals like Brezhnev, but also the role of the Party and its apparatus, as well as the overlapping bureaucracy, generally.

'How successfully' is always a difficult phrase to interpret. It can mean different things to different people. In this context, does 'success' simply mean the ability of the Party to keep itself in power without a threat to its monopolistic position; does it mean the success or otherwise of its management of the economy; does it mean the ability to influence people's attitudes; does it mean the ability to prevent nationalist problems in the republics from coming to the fore? Do you consider the problem from the perspective of those on the receiving end of policies, that is the majority of the population, who were not members of the Party?

These are complex and interesting issues, but you may not be able to cover them all, and you therefore need to plan your arguments carefully, and to define your terms of reference early on. That is why a good plan helps. As with the first question, you may come to a definite conclusion or judgment by the end of your essay, or you may have a qualified answer. The important thing is to have determined your principal approach before you get under way and write the essay.

Source-based questions on *'The Years of Stagnation: Brezhnev's USSR, 1964-82'*

1 Brezhnev on 'Developed Socialism', 1977
Study the extract from Brezhnev's article on page 18 and then answer the following questions:

a) Summarise what Brezhnev meant by 'Developed Socialism'. (3 marks)
b) What arguments did Brezhnev produce to justify his claim that the USSR had achieved 'Developed Socialism'? (4 marks)
c) What was the difference between 'Developed Socialism' and other forms of Socialism and Communism? (4 marks)
d) Use your own knowledge to assess the validity of Brezhnev's claims regarding the economic and political progress of the USSR by the time that this article was written. (5 marks)
e) How useful is this source to historians assessing the economic and political development of the USSR in this period? (4 marks)

2 Criticism of the Dissidents Daniel and Sinyavsky
Study the article on pages 28-9, and then answer the following questions:
a) What arguments are used by the author to criticise Daniel and Sinyavsky and, by implication, other Soviet critics of the regime? (4 marks)
b) Comment on the tone and arguments used to get across the author's viewpoint. (5 marks)
c) How reliable is this source as evidence of Soviet attitudes towards dissidents? (5 marks)
d) Use your own knowledge to assess the significance of dissent in the USSR during the Brezhnev era. (6 marks)

3 The Soviet Economy during the Brezhnev Era
Study the statistics on page 23 and answer the questions which follow:
a) What trends in the Soviet economy are evident from these statistics? (4 marks)
b) Study these statistics in conjunction with Brezhnev's description of 'Developed Socialism' on page 18. To what extent do these two sources support each other? (5 marks)
c) What are the dangers for an historian of using these statistics as evidence of progress or otherwise in the Soviet economy? (4 marks)
d) Use the source and your own knowledge to explain why this period is sometimes called 'a period of economic stagnation' in the USSR. (7 marks)

4 Soviet Propaganda
Study the two posters from the 1970s on page 20 and answer the questions which follow:
a) What is the message of each of these posters? (4 marks)
b) Identify the elements of propaganda in the two posters. (5 marks)
c) How useful are these sources as evidence of government concerns about the Soviet economy in the Brezhnev era? (6 marks)
d) Why should historians of the USSR concern themselves with a study of propaganda? (5 marks)

CHAPTER 3

Foreign Policy under Brezhnev

1 Background

Brezhnev presided over a crucial period in Soviet foreign policy. Although the USSR had emerged as a great power under Stalin, and had broken the American nuclear monopoly at the end of the 1940s, the Soviets found it difficult to compete with the USA in economic and military terms as the Cold War developed. Brezhnev's tenure of power saw several shifts in international relations. Taking over shortly after the Cuban Missile Crisis, Brezhnev sought an improvement in East-West relations, leading to the period known as 'détente'. This was followed by a renewal of tensions during the latter years of his regime. Confrontation, or at least tension, between East and West was always just below the surface, and the situation was complicated by difficult relations with the other developing Communist power, China.

There was a constant theme in Soviet foreign policy during Brezhnev's time in power: a search for a world-wide role both in keeping with Soviet perceptions of the USSR as a great power, and as the leading Marxist state. This involved taking on new commitments outside Soviet borders, and even outside traditionally Russian spheres of influence. However, attempts to maintain or extend Soviet influence outside Eastern Europe frequently failed and, even when successful, provoked international repercussions or, more significantly for the USSR in the long run, imposed enormous strains on the struggling Soviet economy.

The Soviets officially adhered to a policy of peaceful co-existence, which was regarded as the only sensible policy in an era of potential mass destruction. However, there were factions on both sides of the Iron Curtain looking to destabilise their ideological opponents. The USSR itself was committed to propagating the message of the superiority of Socialism: this was to be achieved by demonstrating the advantages of Socialism rather than by trying to impose it on other countries by military force. Competing with the capitalist world, particularly in trying to win the hearts and minds of non-aligned countries, imposed considerable strains on the USSR: being a superpower imposed responsibilities as well as prestige. And superpower status was certainly expensive to maintain. So it proved under Brezhnev, although the real costs of the effort were masked for a long time, until ultimately they began to have a detrimental effect on the economic performance of the USSR, and in particular on the living standards of ordinary people.

Khrushchev's foreign policy had run into difficulties, and his prestige had been dented by the Soviet climb-down in the Cuban Missile Crisis. However, discontent with the Soviet leadership had been as much to do with style as with content: there were many who felt that Khrushchev had cut an undignified figure on the world stage, even if the West had found him a more congenial personality than his predecessor, Stalin. In 1964 there was to be no immediate change of direction in the content of Soviet foreign policy, only a renewed striving for parity with the United States in both the military and diplomatic spheres. This striving was to place the Soviet economy under considerably more strain than the American one, and greatly contributed to the mounting problems within the USSR. Brezhnev was also concerned with consolidating the Socialist bloc and reasserting the USSR's role as leader of the world Communist movement. Waves had been created in Eastern Europe by Khrushchev's policy of de-Stalinisation, and China was contesting Soviet pre-eminence as the torchbearer of Marxism, so an unchanging Soviet leadership could not be taken for granted.

2 Defence and Deterrence

Open conflict with the West was to be avoided wherever possible. Official Soviet policy was emphasised in a Soviet publication in 1971: the aim was:

1 to secure together with the other Socialist countries, favourable conditions for the building of Socialism and Communism, strengthen the unity and solidarity of the Socialist countries, their friendship and brotherhood; support the national-liberation
5 movement and to effect all-round co-operation with the young developing countries; consistently to uphold the principle of peaceful co-existence of states with different social systems, to offer decisive resistance to the aggressive forces of Imperialism and to save mankind from a new world war.

Kosygin, in particular, was keen to improve East-West relations in order to gain more access to Western technology. Nevertheless, there was continuity in Soviet foreign policy, exemplified in the person of Foreign Minister Gromyko, who had been involved in Soviet diplomacy since before the war. The USSR was still committed to helping spread Communist principles throughout the world, although ever since Stalin's day the progress of Communist ideology and the strengthening of Soviet national power had become virtually indistinguishable. Under Gromyko's guidance, the USSR remained cautious, but did continue to increase its military strength and seek tactical advantages during the Cold War when suitable opportunities presented themselves, as they were to do, for example, in Angola and Mozambique, when the Portuguese empire collapsed.

Khrushchev had held to the principle of minimum nuclear deterrence: any foreign power must be convinced that to attack the USSR would not be in its interest, provided that the USSR maintained enough nuclear force to strike a devastating counterblow, even if it were hit first. Brezhnev's regime modified this objective by developing forces capable of matching the USA in different spheres: the ability to wage all-out nuclear war, conventional war, or a limited nuclear war. This latter concept had been developed as a theory by some American strategists, although Soviet military thought maintained that it was not a credible option, in that any use of nuclear weapons would be likely to escalate into all-out war.

Soviet defence spending rose steadily during the 1960s, whilst the amount spent on scientific research for military ends doubled during the decade. Work began in 1966 on an antiballistic missile system based around Moscow. The Soviets were keen to expand their naval power - their inferiority to the Americans in this regard had been very evident during the Cuban Missile Crisis - and they put a Mediterranean squadron into service in 1963, whilst the Soviet navy appeared in the Indian Ocean in 1968. The first Soviet aircraft carrier was launched in 1973 - proof that the navy was being developed for the first time as a long-range instrument of policy. The Soviet air force was also modernised and expanded. East Germany and Czechoslovakia received Soviet help in the updating of their conventional forces.

In 1967 the period of conscription into the Soviet army was reduced from three to two years, but in the following year pre-conscription training became compulsory, in order to ensure a large conventional army that had at least basic military training. Attention was also paid to quality: Khrushchev's policy of reforming the officer corps was continued, meaning that an increasing number of specialists (especially engineer officers) was promoted. However, at the same time as increasing the professionalism of the army, care was taken to strengthen its political reliability and links with the Party: in 1966 93 per cent of all Red Army officers belonged to the Party or the Komsomol.

In 1969 the USSR actually succeeded in overtaking the American lead in strategic nuclear weapons. The USA possessed 656 submarine-launched ballistic missiles compared to the Soviets' 160, and the two powers were roughly comparable in their numbers of intercontinental ballistic missiles (IBMs), but in intermediate-range and other missiles the USSR had a lead. In terms of conventional forces, the Warsaw Pact had 925,000 men under arms compared with 600,000 in NATO forces in northern and central Europe, 12,500 to 5,250 tanks, and 3,795 to 2,050 tactical aircraft. However, a qualitative comparison may have put the Soviets at a disadvantage. Also, although the Soviets were getting to a position where they could negotiate with the Americans on equal terms, it was at the cost of an enormous burden on the Soviet economy. Such was the price of competing with other great powers on the world stage.

3 Détente

Brezhnev was not oblivious to the dangers and the costs of practising a high-profile foreign policy, and accommodation with the West might have proved a more satisfactory policy in the long run than overt competition for influence. However, Soviet-American relations were often poor in the 1960s, the period of Kennedy's and Johnson's presidencies. The USA was heavily involved in the Vietnam War and intervened in Dominica in 1965. Nor were relations helped by the Arab-Israeli war of 1967, since the Arabs were widely seen in the West as the aggressors, and yet the Soviets were friends and suppliers of some Arab states. The Soviet invasion of Czechoslovakia in 1968 also dented the Soviet image, since the Soviet-led operation seemed to be a blatant intervention in the domestic affairs of another state, albeit one which was in the Soviet sphere of influence.

The Soviets in turn were concerned by American activities on the world stage. They became alarmed at what they regarded as American adventurism, particularly since their own relations with China were hostile and they felt isolated. To make matters worse, in 1969 President Nixon launched an American programme to develop MIRVs (multiple independently targetable re-entry vehicles) and an antiballistic missile system. This programme threatened to upset the balance of deterrence, either by giving one side a superiority in weaponry or by forcing the Soviets into more expense in trying to match the American defence effort. The superiority of American technology was confirmed by America's successful moon landing in June 1969.

Brezhnev soon realised the benefits that might accrue from better relationships with the USA and Western Europe - a policy of détente (a relaxation of international tensions). His first public speech included the words: 'The spirit of reckless gambling in the great and serious matter of exploring and mastering space is deeply alien to us'. There were more worldly considerations also: better relations could mean less expenditure on defence. There were examples of co-operation. Both superpowers stayed out of the confrontation between Malaysia and Indonesia, and also the conflict in the Sudan. The Americans supported Soviet mediation in the conflict between India and Pakistan in 1965, and an international crisis over Czechoslovakia was avoided in 1968, despite ill-feeling towards the USSR in the West. Both powers signed a treaty banning nuclear weapons from outer space in 1967, and also a non-proliferation treaty in 1968, by which they committed themselves not to help other powers attain a military nuclear capability. The new mood was helped by Nixon's more cautious approach towards American involvement in the Vietnam War. Also important was the policy of *Ostpolitik* inaugurated by the West German chancellor, Willi Brandt. This opened the prospect of more trading links between East and West, something seen as very important by the Soviets.

Nevertheless, the policy of détente could not be introduced without risks. Brezhnev preferred to avoid confrontation, but he did have to overcome conservative opposition within the Politburo. There was also a concern not to import Western liberalism along with Western technology. It was clear that détente meant a reduction of tension, and possibly arms control, but not disarmament. Nor did it mean that the ideological struggle would be discontinued. Brezhnev declared in 1973:

1 The class struggle of the two systems ... in the sphere of economics, politics, and ... ideology will be continued ... But we shall ensure that this inevitable struggle is transferred to a channel which does not threaten wars, dangerous conflicts and an
5 uncontrollable arms race. (*Pravda*, 5 June 1973.)

Three years later, Brezhnev told the Party Congress:

Détente does not in the slightest abolish, nor can it alter the laws of the class struggle ... We see détente as the way to create more favourable conditions for peaceful Socialist and Communist construction. (Report in *Soviet News*, 2 March 1976.)

In other words, Brezhnev was trying to assure his listeners that the pursuit of détente in no way conflicted with Marxist theories of the class struggle. At the same time, he was attempting a note of realism: thus he had told President Nixon two years earlier that détente was 'irreversible'. Brezhnev could claim that he was pursuing Leninist principles, on the grounds that promoting détente would enable the Soviets to exploit internal divisions within the capitalist world, and possibly foster the growth of foreign Communist parties in a more relaxed international atmosphere.

Kosygin had met President Johnson in July 1967, and had then agreed to discuss the control of nuclear weapons. But détente really got under way in April 1970, when the Strategic Arms Limitation Talks (SALT) began, with the aim of averting an acceleration of the nuclear arms race provoked by the development of MIRVs and ABMs (antiballistic missiles). In February 1971 the USSR, USA and Britain signed an agreement banning the installation of nuclear devices on the sea bed; and in September the two superpowers agreed to convert the hot line between the Kremlin and Washington into a satellite communications system and to take measures to deal with accidental missile launches. The USSR was particularly anxious to conclude more agreements, because Nixon's visit to China in May 1972 opened up the prospect of a Sino-American *rapprochement* which would leave the USSR isolated.

In the same month as Nixon's visit to China, the USSR and USA signed a series of agreements on environmental protection, the use of outer space, health, science and technology, and the basic principles of mutual relations, in which the two powers agreed to work towards the prevention of crises and war, a limitation on offensive weapons, and the promotion of mutual cultural, economic and technical links. Further commercial links were established, including the much publicised granting of a licence to Moscow to produce Pepsi-Cola in the USSR.

An ABM treaty limited each power to two ABM sites, each site containing 100 missiles, to protect the country's capital city; and one ICBM site, so as to reduce the possibility of a surprise attack intended to destroy the enemy's capacity to retaliate. A five-year agreement placed a ceiling on the deployment of land-based strategic missiles. The USSR would have more ICBMs, but the Americans would have more MIRVs. Limitations were also placed on the development of SLBMs (submarine-launched ballistic missiles).

Brezhnev acquired considerable prestige from these agreements, known as the SALT I agreements, but he did not rest upon his laurels. The USSR immediately signed further agreements with several West European countries, with the notable exception of Britain, with whom relations were strained. In December 1972 Moscow signed a trade agreement with Spain. The Kremlin also cultivated France: Moscow was apprehensive about the development of the European Economic Community as a major force in Europe, and regarded French nationalist feeling as a potentially disruptive force within that institution. A non-aggression treaty between the USSR and West Germany had already been signed in 1970, and commercial relations between the two countries were expanding. In December 1972 a treaty between the two Germanies was signed, followed in May 1973 by a ten-year agreement on technical co-operation between the USSR and West Germany. Brezhnev was also keen to hold a European security conference to validate the division of Europe and achieve full recognition of the status of East Germany. In return for this, the Soviets agreed to a parallel conference on mutual and balanced force reductions at Vienna, to begin in October 1973. Talks were initiated, but they were to drag on for the rest of the decade without an agreement being reached.

In August 1973 the USSR and 32 other European states, plus the USA and Canada, signed the Helsinki Act of the European Security Conference. Frontiers were recognised; prior notice was to be given before the holding of large-scale military manoeuvres; economic and environmental co-operation was also to be promoted. Human rights on thought, conscience and religion were guaranteed. There were also guarantees to national minorities; and in addition cultural exchanges were to be furthered.

Brezhnev had achieved a great deal in real terms for the USSR, but the human-rights emphasis was to prove an embarrassment, since Helsinki monitoring groups were set up throughout Eastern Europe and they complained about Soviet violations. A Helsinki review conference held in Belgrade in the winter of 1977-8 brought international criticism of the USSR, especially from the new American president, Jimmy Carter. Nevertheless, Soviet relations with most Western countries remained reasonably cordial, and trade between them and the USSR increased steadily, reaching a peak in 1979. Relations with Japan were also improved.

Brezhnev hoped for a SALT II treaty to maintain the momentum of détente. Arms-control talks were complicated by technical developments, notably of MIRVs and the development in the West of cruise missiles, difficult to detect on radar, and the neutron bomb; whilst the Soviets were developing a new bomber. Nevertheless, the SALT II Treaty was signed in Vienna in June 1979. It limited both superpowers to 2,250 strategic missiles and 1,320 MIRVs.

However, ratification of the treaty did not take place. Instead, mutual suspicion grew. The USA was alarmed at the stationing of Soviet troops in Cuba, whilst the USSR in turn was alarmed by NATO's decision in December 1979 to deploy several hundred short- and medium-range missiles in Europe. The West was unimpressed by the Soviet withdrawal of 20,000 troops and 1,000 tanks from East Germany during 1979 and 1980. Suspicions were further heightened by the Soviet invasion of Afghanistan in December 1979.

However, détente was already dying well before the Soviet invasion. Sections of the American establishment had rejected détente back in 1976. Carter stepped up the arms race, and by December 1978 was demanding a big increase in the military budget. In December 1979 NATO decided to deploy long-range missiles in Europe. Some American supporters of a new arms race argued that the Soviets had been using détente as a cover to extend their influence in the Third, or developing, World, and were actually attempting to achieve a first-strike nuclear capability. This was not true, but a Soviet threat did appear real, because during the 1970s a number of Western-sponsored regimes fell to radical movements - in Vietnam, Angola, Mozambique, Ethiopia, Iran, Nicaragua and South Yemen. The USSR may have appeared to benefit politically from these revolts, since the latter succeeded largely because of inadequacies in Western policy, but Washington was simplistic in putting most of the blame for these events on a policy of Soviet subversion.

The belief in Soviet expansionism was also held by President Reagan. He declared in 1980 that the Soviets, along with the Cubans, were responsible for revolts in El Salvador and the rest of Central America. The Americans continued to make innovations in military technology, and by the early 1980s had 360 major bases and over 1,000 major installations in 36 countries. Reagan enthusiastically pursued 'Star Wars', or the Strategic Defence Initiative, designed both to deter the Soviets from aggression, and to provide the USA with protection. The Soviets tried to respond to these American initiatives by developing their

Soviet Cold War cartoon: 'Guiding Star'

Soviet Cold War cartoon: 'Voice of the Dictator'

own defence programme and facilities. However, Soviet efforts were mostly ineffectual, and during Brezhnev's time the Soviets had the use of only 15 foreign ports.

4 A Global Strategy

The Americans had adopted a world-wide role since the ending of World War II. Brezhnev's USSR assumed such a role too, although it was less well-equipped to carry it out successfully. Brezhnev certainly continued and extended some of Khrushchev's policies, for example, supporting Socialist and nationalist movements in the developing world. Soviet aid was usually military, as the USSR could not afford the vast amounts of economic aid which the USA often made available. However, COMECON (the Council for Mutual Economic Assistance), although essentially an Eastern European organisation, was extended to include Cuba and Vietnam, at great cost. One problem with Soviet strategy was that it was not always possible to convert military aid into political influence.

In Vietnam, Brezhnev was more enthusiastic than Khrushchev had been about supporting the Communist cause. It was a useful means both of supporting a Communist neighbour and embarrassing the United States. The Communist leader, Ho Chi Minh, was a trained Soviet agent. In 1965 the Soviets publicly promised aid to the Hanoi regime and did provide it between 1965 and 1971. Soviet aid was arguably responsible for the rapid North Vietnamese advance of the early 1970s. Although the Soviets did not exert great influence over the North Vietnamese, the war did have the advantage for them of tying up large amounts of American wealth, and caused considerable embarrassment to the USA both at home and in its relations with many other countries. Following the ending of the war, the by then united Vietnam signed a treaty of friendship and co-operation with the Kremlin. The Soviets furthermore tried to use Vietnam as a counterweight against China in Southeast Asia.

Brezhnev took up opportunities to extend Soviet influence elsewhere. He continued Khrushchev's policy of giving aid to African countries. For example, Soviet aid was important to the rebel movement in Angola. The Soviets also established a base in Somalia and trained the Somali army, although when the Somalis attacked Ethiopia in 1977, the regime there was supported by the Kremlin, suggesting that there was some confusion about Soviet policy.

In South America, the limitations of Soviet influence were demonstrated in 1973, when the Marxist president of Chile, Allende, was overthrown in a coup. The Soviets could do little but criticise the United States for destabilising Allende's regime. The Soviets could still not compete effectively with the USA on a global basis, since outside Europe they simply lacked the political, economic or military clout with which to challenge American supremacy.

After Khrushchev's fall from power the Soviets tried to woo India as an ally. Kosygin mediated between India and Pakistan following the war between them in 1965. The Soviets also supplied India with arms. The two counties signed a treaty of friendship and co-operation in 1971, which was renewed in 1976. This was also part of the Soviet strategy to contain China, seen as a threat by the Indians as well as by the Soviets. However, following Mao's death, relations between India and China improved, consequently loosening the ties between India and the USSR.

5 The Middle East

The Middle East, being close geographically to the USSR, was of even greater interest to the Soviets. Many Arab states which would almost certainly have been hostile to the Marxist philosophy of the USSR, nevertheless sought Soviet aid during the long-running dispute between the Arab world and Israel. However, Moscow's credibility with the Arabs was severely dented by the Arab humiliation during the Arab-Israeli Six-day War of 1967, and diplomatic initiatives after the war passed to the Western powers and the United Nations.

In 1971 the USSR began to re-equip Egypt with modern weapons. However, the Egyptians were not convinced of the value of Soviet support, and Egypt's President Sadat ordered the Soviets out of Egypt in July 1972. Although there was a *rapprochement* within months, Soviet influence in both Egypt and Syria was declining.

During the renewed Arab-Israeli War of 1973, the proximity of American and Soviet fleets in the Mediterranean brought about a nuclear alert and the danger of a major confrontation between the superpowers, as serious as the events in Cuba a decade earlier. Although the Soviets tried to maintain their influence in the region, Sadat was now more interested in using American influence to bring about a peace settlement. When the historic Camp David Peace Agreement was signed between Egypt and Israel, the Soviets poured scorn upon it, but the agreement put America rather than the USSR at the centre of the Middle-Eastern stage. Consequently, when Brezhnev warned the Americans in 1982 to keep out of the Lebanon, currently racked by civil war and instability, he was ignored. The Soviets continued to support Syria, and showed an interest in solving the Palestinian problem, but they were careful not to provoke the USA. The message was clear: although the Middle East was far closer to the Soviet than the American borders, precisely because it was an area in which the Americans felt they had a direct political and strategic interest, it proved impossible for the weaker USSR to make the running in diplomatic initiatives.

6 Afghanistan

The limitations of Soviet foreign policy under Brezhnev were nowhere more cruelly exposed than in Afghanistan. Afghanistan had historically been a place of strategic interest to Russia, long before the Russian Revolution. The Communists now appeared to be making gains there. However, a Marxist coup in 1978 lasted less than two years before the coup's leader, Taraki, and his Soviet advisers were overthrown. Soviet troops invaded Afghanistan in December 1979, ostensibly at the request of the threatened government in Kabul. By April 1980 there were 100,000 Soviet troops in Afghanistan. It was the first time that the Red Army had crossed the Iron Curtain since 1945. Moscow was afraid of Muslim fundamentalism spreading from Iran through Afghanistan into its own Muslim republics. There was also the possibility of an extension of Soviet influence towards a warm-water port on the Indian Ocean. Brezhnev's explanation of the invasion was straightforward:

> 1 to have acted otherwise would have meant ... permitting a
> repetition of what aggressive forces succeeded in doing - for
> example - in Chile ... looking on passively while the source of a
> serious threat to the security of the Soviet Union arose on our
> 5 southern border. (*Pravda*, 13 January 1980.)

A longer justification for Soviet intervention in Afghanistan appeared later in 1980:

> 1 Developments forced us to make a choice: we had either to bring in
> troops or let the Afghan revolution be defeated and the country
> turned into a kind of shah's Iran. We decided to bring in the
> troops. It was not a simple decision to take. We weighed the pros
> 5 and cons before taking it. We knew that the victory of
> counter-revolution and of religious zealots and revenge-seeking
> feudal lords would result in a bloodbath before which even the
> crimes of the Chilean junta would pale. We knew that the victory of
> counter-revolution would pave the way for massive American
> 10 military presence in a country which borders on the Soviet Union
> and that this was a challenge to our country's security. We knew
> that the decision to bring in troops would not be popular in the
> modern world even if it was absolutely legal. But we also knew that
> we would have ceased to be a great power if we refrained from
> 15 carrying the burden of taking unpopular but necessary decisions,
> extraordinary decisions prompted by extraordinary circumstances
> ... There are situations when non-intervention is a disgrace and a
> betrayal. Such a situation developed in Afghanistan. And when I
> hear the voices of protest from people who claim to be democrats,

20 humanists and even revolutionaries, saying they are outraged by Soviet 'intervention' I tell them this: it is logic that prompted us. If you are against Soviet military aid to Afghanistan, then you are for the victory of counter-revolution. There is no third way.
Bovin in *Izvestia*, April 1980.

The Afghan adventure was to be a painful experience for the Soviets, a drain on its manpower and wealth. In addition, the strength of the anti-Soviet reaction in the West and the developing world appeared to take the Kremlin by surprise. The USA imposed a boycott on exports of grain and technology to the USSR, and some countries boycotted the 1980 Moscow Olympics. Media reporting of the war was limited, but nevertheless dissatisfaction within the USSR at the material and psychological cost of the war developed. As the casualty lists lengthened, it proved impossible to hide the draining effect of the war from the population, in spite of official censorship. Adverse reaction to Soviet involvement in the war, expressed openly in other countries, and less overtly within the USSR itself, was a stimulus to the new thinking on foreign policy which would develop under Gorbachev later in the 1980s.

7 Eastern Europe and the Brezhnev Doctrine

The USSR had shown its determination to maintain control over its Eastern European sphere of influence in 1956, when Soviet tanks had crushed the Hungarian Rising. Moscow would not tolerate ideological deviations which might threaten the stability of the Warsaw Pact and its own defences. The Warsaw Pact had developed a consultative and command system which attempted to bind the armies of the Eastern bloc closer together. Soviet influence was dominant, since the commander was always Soviet, and the Pact's high command was integrated with the Soviet defence structure.

When Czechoslovakia began to liberalise its regime in 1968 under the new leader, Alexander Dubček, the Soviets feared a trend which might spread throughout the Eastern bloc. Moscow had originally welcomed Dubček's appointment in January 1968, but Soviet attitudes changed as the pace of reform quickened, and there was even talk of the Czechoslovaks leaving the Warsaw Pact. The Pact held military exercises near the Czech border, and Kosygin visited Prague in May 1968. The Czechoslovaks were warned about their activities. A meeting between Dubček and the Soviet Politburo solved little, and showed Brezhnev at his worst, bullying and insulting the Czechoslovak leader. On 20 August Soviet and other Warsaw Pact forces invaded Czechoslovakia. The reforms were dismantled, and Dubček was replaced as Czech leader in April 1969.

The USSR was condemned for its actions in the West, the developing world, and even within parts of the Communist world. However,

Moscow was unrepentant. In November 1968 the 'Brezhnev Doctrine' was issued. Moscow reserved the right to interfere in other Socialist states in the interests of Socialism:

1 When internal and external forces hostile to Socialism attempt to turn the development of any Socialist country in the direction of the capitalist system, when a threat arises to the cause of Socialism in that country, a threat to the security of the Socialist
5 commonwealth as a whole - it already becomes not only a problem for the people of that country, but also a general problem, the concern of all Socialist countries ... The sovereignty of each Socialist country cannot be opposed to the interests of the world of Socialism, of the world revolutionary movement. Lenin demanded
10 that all Communists fight against small-nation narrowmindedness, seclusion and isolation, consider the whole and the general, subordinate the particular to the general interest ... this means, first of all, that, in its activity, each Communist party cannot but take into account such a decisive fact of our time as the struggle
15 between two opposing social systems - capitalism and Socialism. ... There is no doubt that the actions of the five allied Socialist countries in Czechoslovakia directed to the defence of the vital interests of the Socialist community, and the sovereignty of Socialist Czechoslovakia first and foremost, will be increasingly
20 supported by all those who have the interest of the present revolutionary movement, of peace and security of peoples, of democracy and Socialism at heart.

Despite the outrage expressed in many countries at the invasion of Czechoslovakia, there was no question of their intervening against Soviet actions. It was accepted that Czechoslovakia was within the Soviet sphere of influence. The Brezhnev Doctrine did serve as a warning to other Communist states. When there were demands for reform in Poland in 1980, prompted by the Solidarity movement, the threat of Soviet intervention was enough to make the Polish Communist leadership take strong measures to curb the radicals.

There were difficulties with Romania, which pursued an independent line in its foreign relations, for example, by maintaining close ties with China, but this was tolerated, partly because the Romanian leadership maintained a strict anti-reformist stance at home.

During the Brezhnev years, Eastern Europe was in some respects becoming less dependent upon the USSR. Some of the Eastern European states signed treaties with the West Germans, and in several instances the economies of Eastern European states were becoming less dependent on the USSR, and were creating more ties with the non-Communist world. Nevertheless, the Brezhnev Doctrine was always in the background as a threat to those regimes which might go against Moscow's perceived interests. This situation was to continue until Gorbachev buried the doctrine several years later.

8 China

China remained a thorny problem for the Soviets under Brezhnev. Relations had been broken off in Khrushchev's day, and the Chinese were going down their own path to Socialism, whilst condemning their former Soviet mentors as 'revisionists' who had forgotten their Marxist principles. It was not just a question of hurt pride: the Soviets also feared a strategic threat from a large and ambitious China with long-standing territorial claims on portions of the former Russian empire.

Attempts by Brezhnev to improve relations between the USSR and China failed dismally. Serious thought was given in Moscow to the possibility of a pre-emptive nuclear strike to eliminate China's infant nuclear capability. In 1969 there were serious clashes on the Sino-Soviet border, and the Chinese branded the Soviets a 'revisionist' power. By 1980 there were 46 Soviet divisions stationed along the border with China. Further clashes occurred in 1972 and 1974. After Mao's death relations were less strained, but China was still unwilling to return to the Soviet fold, particularly after the Soviet invasion of Aghanistan. Consequently Moscow looked to Vietnam rather than China as its chief ally in Asia.

9 Superpower Status and its Costs

Despite criticism of Khrushchev's foreign policy, he had begun a strategy which enabled the Soviets to pursue global ambitions. A strong military capability was regarded as essential, both for defence and deterrence, and to prevent the USA from dictating the course of world events. The USSR maintained large conventional as well as nuclear forces, and Brezhnev pleased the military by clearly respecting its professional expertise.

The drawback of Brezhnev's strategy was that it required massive defence spending. By 1980 the USSR was spending about 12 per cent of its gross national product on defence, at a time when the economy was slowing down. That was over twice the percentage of the USA and Western European states. By the time of Brezhnev's death, the USSR maintained a global strategic capability and nuclear parity with the USA, but at the cost of a limited range of consumer goods in Soviet shops. The USSR was in danger of being overextended by its commitments: troops and missiles were being maintained in central Europe, central Asia and the Far East. The Soviets had no reliable allies outside the Warsaw Pact, although Moscow did acquire friends or bases in Cuba, Vietnam, North Korea, Afghanistan, South Yemen and Syria.

The Soviets' own efforts to prevent Japan and China from achieving closer relations with the USA were unsuccessful. The USSR also failed in its efforts to drive a wedge between the USA and its Western European allies. The USSR lacked the economic muscle to back up its international ambitions, and its external influence was often restricted by domestic difficulties. Soviet citizens paid the price for their leaders' ambitions, and the resulting domestic stagnation forced Brezhnev's successors to grasp the nettle of fundamental reform and new thinking in both domestic and foreign policy.

Making notes on *'Foreign Policy under Brezhnev'*

Your notes should help you to understand the way in which Soviet foreign policy developed during the Brezhnev years: the growing commitments and examples of Soviet intervention world-wide; the successes and failures of Soviet foreign policy; and the impact it had upon East-West relations and upon the USSR itself. The following headings, subheadings and questions should help you.

1   Background
1.1 What were Brezhnev's aims in foreign policy in 1964?
2   Defence and deterrence
2.1 How did Soviet foreign and defence policy develop in the late 1960s?
2.2 Developments in military thinking and strategy during the Brezhnev years
2.3 How did the USSR compare with the West in military capability?
3   Détente
3.1 Soviet motives for détente
3.2 The SALT talks and arms control
3.3 The Helsinki Agreement
3.4 The breakdown of détente
4   A global strategy
4.1 Soviet policy towards Vietnam
4.2 Soviet policy in Africa
4.3 Soviet influence in South America
4.4 Soviet policy towards India
5   The Middle East
5.1 How successful was Soviet policy in the Middle East?
6   Afghanistan
6.1 Soviet motives for invading Afghanistan
6.2 The impact of the war in Afghanistan
7   Eastern Europe and the Brezhnev Doctrine
7.1 The Soviet invasion of Czechoslovakia in 1968
7.2 The significance of the Brezhnev Doctrine
8   China

8.1 Sino-Soviet relations
9   Superpower status and its costs
9.1 The effect of Soviet foreign policy on Brezhnev's USSR

Answering essay questions on 'Foreign Policy under Brezhnev'

Questions specifically on Soviet foreign policy at this time are likely to be general ones, covering the whole period 1964 to 1982. There are unlikely to be questions relating to specific aspects or countries, unless it is a question relating to Soviet relations with the West, or one relating to détente. There may be a question relating to Eastern Europe. Brezhnev's foreign policy may come into a general question on the Soviet Union during these years, in which case you would also need to make use of the information in Chapter 2.

The fundamental questions relating to Soviet foreign policy are likely to be related to the following themes: (a) What were the aims of Soviet foreign policy in these years? (b) How successful was Soviet foreign policy? (c) To what extent did Soviet foreign policy and domestic policy interact?

These themes are, of course, inter-related. It is impossible to measure the success of a policy without understanding something of its aims, although there is more than that involved. Analysing the relationship of external and internal events also obliges you to consider issues of motives and success.

Consider the following examination questions:

1   How successful was Soviet foreign policy under Brezhnev?
2   'The failure of détente was also the biggest failure of Soviet foreign policy.' To what extent is this a valid assessment of Soviet foreign policy under Brezhnev?
3   Analyse the success of the Soviet Union in maintaining its position as a world power during the Brezhnev years (1964-82).

As before, it is suggested that you approach these essays in the following way: firstly, identify the key words in the title; then decide upon your main theme and plan accordingly; then complete the introduction, main body of the essay, and your conclusion.

The key words in essay number one are 'How successful'. In order to give a complete answer, you need to consider several factors: what was the status of the USSR in world affairs and how successful was its foreign policy at the time of Brezhnev's accession to power in 1964; what were the aims of Soviet foreign policy at that time; were those aims constant or did they change at all during the next 18 years; and to what extent had the Soviets achieved their objectives by the time of Brezhnev's death in 1982?

You will then need to plan the main theme of your essay. There may be several aspects to this. You may take the line that the USSR was a superpower in 1964, in that it did have considerable influence on the world stage, and that this was still the situation in 1982, although the strains of maintaining this position were beginning to show, particularly on the economy. Likewise, you may wish to argue that if one of the main aims of Soviet foreign policy was to achieve parity with the USA, it did achieve this in military terms, and certainly achieved nuclear parity.

When analysing Soviet influence in particular parts of the world, the picture becomes more complex. Using the material in this chapter, you may wish to take the line that Soviet policy failed in several areas: in attempting to extend Soviet influence significantly in Asia and Africa; in failing to achieve lasting progress in détente; in failing to solve the long dispute with China or to win recognition as leader of the world Communist movement. On the other hand, there was limited progress on arms control, and the USSR did, with some difficulty, maintain its influence in Eastern and central Europe, although all the time internal pressures were taking their toll on the Soviet economy, and these pressures brought about changes after Brezhnev's death.

Whatever your line of argument, you should not simply *describe* Soviet actions, but *analyse* Soviet foreign policy in terms of its aims and successes as outlined above. Finally, you should summarise your arguments in your conclusion, whatever it is.

Question number two appears more complex, at least at first sight. There are several key words or phrases to be considered: 'failure of détente', 'biggest failure of Soviet foreign policy', 'valid assessment'.

In planning your response to these key words, it is a good idea to make your terms of reference very clear. In this case, define 'détente', and give a brief summary of its main features during these years - its progress and then its decline.

Then you should consider the main thrust of the question. The question implies that détente was an important objective of Soviet foreign policy. This point should be discussed, and you should decide what Brezhnev's objectives were, and why détente was an important policy to the Soviets.

The final part of the question requires careful thought. You will need to consider some of the same material as was already covered in essay number one. In other words, what were the other failures of Soviet foreign policy at this time? Were they as significant as the failure of détente? How important was the failure of détente, not so much for the rest of the world but for the USSR?

It is important that you decide on your approach at the planning stage, since your essay should have a coherent theme, which is brought together in the conclusion, whatever the extent of your agreement or otherwise with the quotation.

Question number three contains many elements already covered in essays number one and two. The key words here are 'analyse' and 'world power'. 'Analyse' means 'examine critically', not 'describe what happened'. You should also decide what is meant by 'world power' (political, economic or military factors, or a combination of all three) and whether this is an accurate description of the USSR in either 1964 or 1982.

Clearly you should be able to assess the influence of the USSR on the world stage at different times. You will probably examine the consequences of Khrushchev's climb-down over Cuba, and the determination of the Soviets to build up their military capacity in order to compete with the USA on a global basis. You are likely to include much of the same material as in essay number one. You might argue that the USSR was more successful in achieving its objectives in some areas (for example Eastern Europe) than in others.

Again, your definition of 'success' is very important. You may take the line that, despite all its efforts, the USSR failed to compete successfully with the USA. On the other hand, the USSR was closely involved in world affairs and major issues like détente; was always regarded as one of the influential powers with which to be reckoned; and its position as a nuclear power ensured that it would always remain in the first rank. Alternatively, if your argument is that the USSR suffered a perceptible decline in its influence during these years, you should examine why this was, also considering domestic factors such as economic difficulties.

As with the other essays, you should decide on your theme at the planning stage, so that your argument has a coherent thread, supported by relevant evidence, from the introduction, through the main body of the essay, to the conclusion.

Source-based questions on 'Foreign Policy under Brezhnev'

1 Anti-American Attitudes
Study the two cartoons on page 41 and answer the following questions:
a) What is the message portrayed in the two cartoons? (4 marks)
b) What techniques are used to get across the message? (5 marks)
c) How reliable are these sources as evidence of Cold War attitudes? (5 marks)
d) What are the uses and limitations of these sources as evidence of Soviet Cold War attitudes? (6 marks)

2 Soviet Intervention in Afghanistan
Study the extract on pages 44-5 and answer the following questions:
a) Explain the references to 'Afghan revolution' and the 'shah's Iran'. (4 marks)
b) What arguments are used in this extract to justify Soviet intervention in Afghanistan? (5 marks)

c) What techniques are used by the author to strengthen his arguments? (5 marks)
d) Using your own knowledge, examine the extent to which the arguments and tone of this source were typical of the Soviet approach to international relations in the Cold War era. (6 marks)

3 The Brezhnev Doctrine
Study Brezhnev's pronouncements on the Brezhnev Doctrine on page 46 and answer the following questions:
a) Using your own knowledge, explain the reference in lines 16-17 to 'the actions of the five allied Socialist countries in Czechoslovakia.' (4 marks)
b) What, according to Brezhnev, was the Brezhnev Doctrine? (4 marks)
c) What justification did Brezhnev give for the principle of intervention? (4 marks)
d) Identify the elements of propaganda in this source. (4 marks)
e) Compare the arguments for intervention in this source with those in the source on pages 44-5 justifying Soviet intervention in Afghanistan. (4 marks)

CHAPTER 4

The Andropov-Chernenko Interregnum, 1982-5

1 The Succession to Brezhnev

Brezhnev had been in power for so long that many younger people in the USSR could not remember another leader. The long time span of his regime had contributed greatly to an atmosphere of stability which had masked many of the growing economic problems. As Brezhnev's health waned, so the period of stability ended, and his successors had to face up to serious problems, whilst conducting their own power struggles. The short-lived regimes of Brezhnev's successors were to signify a period of uncertainty, but were also important in determining the future direction of the USSR.

Brezhnev was clearly in poor health at the opening of the Olympic Games in Moscow in 1980. His speech and movements were slow, and it was known that he had visited a faith healer. His health remained poor, and after flying to Tashkent in March 1982, he suffered a stroke. In the previous year he had attended his last Party Congress, the twenty-eighth. At that Congress he gave a franker than usual assessment of Soviet prospects. He told his audience that because of domestic problems and an unfavourable world economic situation, it would take longer to attain the Communist ideal than had been anticipated. He listed economic failings, shortages of food and consumer goods, a poor health service, alcoholism, a breakdown in family values, and hooliganism as the reasons. He did not add that his own failure to take decisive action had been partly responsible for this situation, and he offered no real solutions, which was in keeping with much of what had gone before.

During 1982 Brezhnev's health was so poor that his speeches had to be edited and doctored for the television news in order to disguise his slurred delivery. One of his last pronouncements was in October: an attack on the American 'political, ideological and economic offensive against Socialism'. This speech was prompted by criticism from Soviet generals concerned about the possibility of cuts in the arms programme and by attempts to woo the Chinese.

Andropov prepared an exhausting work schedule for the dying leader. Rumours abounded that Andropov was trying to finish Brezhnev off in order to facilitate his own succession. In September 1982, in Baku, Brezhnev was suddenly presented with a speech to read publicly, one different from that which he had expected. In November he was made to stand in Red Square for two hours in sub-zero temperatures to witness the annual military parade on the anniversary of the Revolution. Both events added to the rumours.

Brezhnev's death was announced on 11 November. Because it was not unexpected, the mood throughout the USSR was quiet, almost one of anti-climax. Brezhnev's successor, Yuri Andropov, was appointed general secretary almost immediately. It appeared to have been a smooth operation. The Politburo met before the Central Committee did, and although Prime Minister Tikhonov nominated Konstantin Chernenko for the leadership, Marshal Ustinov announced that a decision had already been taken in favour of Andropov. It was effectively a bloodless coup by the military and the KGB.

The important question was: would the forces of conservatism which had dominated the Kremlin for the previous 18 years continue to hold sway, or would those who recognised the need for reform get their chance? The question was soon answered, at least in Andropov's domestic policy.

2 The Rise of Yuri Andropov

Yuri Andropov was almost entirely unknown outside the USSR, and even within the country his name meant little to most people. His tenure as general secretary was to be brief, but significant, chiefly because several of his ideas were later to be carried forward by his own chosen successor, Mikhail Gorbachev, after a brief period of retrenchment under Chernenko. Gorbachev's own rise to prominence would probably have been much more difficult without the patronage of Andropov.

Andropov was the son of a railwayman from the north Caucasus, and he left school in 1930, at the age of 16. He became a Komsomol, or Young Communist, leader in the north Caucasus and at Yaroslavl. During World War II, he served in Karelia, near the Finnish border. Then marked out for promotion, he began a diplomatic career by becoming Soviet ambassador to Hungary.

Andropov was in Hungary during the brutal Soviet suppression of the 1956 rising. This experience was important: it was Andropov who recommended to Moscow that the new Hungarian leader should be the relatively moderate János Kádár. Andropov's experience of later Hungarian economic experiments, liberal by Communist standards and less dependent upon central controls, would influence his own attitude towards reform.

By 1957 Andropov was on the Central Committee. He maintained contacts with Soviet personnel in several foreign countries, and this gave him a different and broader perspective on political and economic issues from that of some of his associates.

Andropov was promoted again after the fall of Khrushchev, and formed the Fifth Directorate of the KGB in 1968. Its task was to suppress dissent in all its manifestations - political, nationalist, cultural and religious. But Andropov was also one of a newer breed of KGB leaders. He wanted Party control of the security services, and he emphasised the importance of legal procedures. He stated that he wished to persuade dissidents that their activities harmed the Soviet state. He was not interested in blind repression for its own sake. As head of the KGB, an appointment made in May 1967, he received accurate reports about the true state of affairs both at home and abroad, and therefore when he became general secretary he was probably more knowledgeable than any previous Soviet leader, and less likely to be taken in by the regime's own propaganda.

With this background, it is not surprising that even Andropov's earliest speeches criticised the shortcomings of Soviet bureaucracy. Naturally he was firmly committed to the Party, and was orthodox in most of his views, but he was not blind to the problems around him. As an intelligent realist, he recognised the need for reform. This did not make him a liberal. Indeed, Andropov believed that the USSR must remain on guard in its ideological confrontation with the West, and he could be ruthless when he thought it necessary. For example, it was Andropov who exiled the dissident physicist Andrei Sakharov to Gorky in 1980, and it may have been he who ordered an assassination attempt on Pope John Paul II in May 1981.

Andropov's ambition certainly embraced a desire to succeed the ailing Brezhnev. The KGB spread rumours during 1982 that Brezhnev was about to retire, and Andropov relinquished his KGB post in May 1982. This may have been a tactical move: it had always been accepted that no head of the KGB could become general secretary. Andropov was put in charge of ideology, but he continued to use his recent KGB influence to undermine both Brezhnev and his own successor, Chernenko. He was supported in this by the powerful defence minister, Marshal Ustinov, and Foreign Minister Gromyko. Andropov disassociated himself from Brezhnev's failures, and as a means of undermining him further, he conducted a well-publicised campaign against Brezhnev's daughter, Galina, who was involved in corruption and the Soviet underworld.

Little was known about Andropov other than his work. He was a very private man, and remained so when in power. He was regarded as being an austere, personally modest, demanding individual, with intellectual leanings and a liking for music and art. As he became more prominent in the political world, the Western press, anxious to know more about him, painted a picture of a secret liberal, with a love of Western jazz and modern art. This distorted image was fostered by Soviet propaganda, for foreign-policy purposes. More importantly, the West confused realism with liberalism, finding it difficult to accept that a reformer could wish to change things without challenging the system itself. But this was precisely Andropov's intention: to reform whilst maintaining the essential orthodoxies of the Soviet system. In this respect Andropov was following in the footsteps of Khrushchev, and anticipating Gorbachev in the early years of the latter's tenure of power.

Andropov certainly impressed those foreigners who met him. He appeared somewhat aloof, but commanded respect. He was also regarded by colleagues far more highly than the ageing Chernenko, the man who had been at Brezhnev's side and who had been expected to succeed him. But after Brezhnev's death, Chernenko was forced to concede primacy to Andropov.

3 Discipline and Reform

Andropov began his tenure of office with vigour, immediately launching a twin assault on Brezhnev's close supporters and the perceived ills in the Soviet economy and society. Efficiency and discipline were the new catchwords. Andropov attacked 'anti-Soviet actions which arouse popular indignation'. He was determined to root out corruption and abuse of privilege. However, many citizens were soon alarmed by his methods. These included the setting up of 'People's Control', an inspectorate whose members, accompanied by the police, went around shops, cinemas and cafés questioning people about why they were not at work. The reason for Andropov's actions was clear: an official report in 1982 revealed that for every 100 Soviets of work age, 30 were absent from work at any one time for 'personal reasons'. Alcoholism was one reason among many others for this. It was a classic Soviet dilemma: the need for action was obvious - there were also severe food shortages late in 1982 - but drastic reform measures aroused hostility if they disrupted established patterns of life, or threatened those who profited from the system. Andropov's stark messages, 'There are no miracles', and 'Without discipline we cannot advance quickly', were pertinent, as was his message that improvements in wages, working and living conditions could only come from hard work and greater productivity. But they were difficult messages for many Soviets to stomach without evidence of immediate benefits.

In order to implement his policies, Andropov put his own team in place. The usual change of personnel in the Politburo and ministries occurred when a new man took over, and there were also changes at management level in industry. Andropov did not make himself president for another eight months, possibly from a concern that he might arouse too much opposition: the Brezhnevites still had a foothold in power, and were spreading rumours that Brezhnev had nominated Chernenko as his successor in his will. Nevertheless, Andropov did promote some of his younger protégés. Nikolai Ryzhkov was made the Central Committee secretary responsible for a new economic programme. Grigori Romanov was put in charge of heavy industry. Mikhail Gorbachev, at 52, was the only representative of the younger political generation in the Politburo. He was one of those frustrated at the conservatism of the old hands who had been at the helm for years. Andropov also had the support of Gromyko. Gromyko was a symbol of continuity with the past, and was

greatly respected for his shrewdness and experience, but he was not
regarded as a political threat because he had no substantial power base
within the Party.

Domestic reform was high on Andropov's agenda. At the end of 1982
Pravda was used to attack abuses and failings in the economic system,
and to suggest reforms such as the setting up of smaller enterprises; and
it insisted that sectors such as transport must demonstrate higher
productivity if they were to continue to receive substantial state funding.
Already in November 1982 the new general secretary had delivered a
forceful speech to the Central Committee, combining calls for
discipline, reform and ideological commitment.

1 Labour productivity is growing at rates that cannot satisfy us. The
lack of co-ordination in the development of the raw materials and
processing branches remains a problem ... Plans continue to be
fulfilled at the cost of large outlays and production expenses.
5 There are still a good many economic managers who, while glibly
quoting Leonid Ilyich's [Brezhnev] maxim that the economy
should be economical, are in reality doing little to accomplish this
task. Apparently the force of inertia and old habits are still at work.
And some people, perhaps, simply don't know how to tackle the
10 job ... The main thing is to accelerate work to improve the entire
sphere of economic management - administration, planning and
the economic mechanism ... Conversely, poor work, sluggishness
and irresponsibility should have an immediate and inescapable
effect   on the remuneration, job status and moral prestige of
15 personnel (Applause) ... We must wage a more resolute struggle
against all violations of Party, state and labour discipline. I'm
certain that in this we will have the full support of Party and trade
union   organisations   and   the   support   of   all   Soviet   people
(Applause) ... In general, slogans alone won't get things moving.
20 Large-scale organisational work by Party organisations, economic
managers and engineering and technical personnel is needed if
every one of these vast and important tasks is to be examined in the
context not only of each branch but also of every plant, every shop
and work sector and, if you will, every workplace.
Speech to the Central Committee of the CPSU, 23 November
1982.

In August 1983 Andropov told a conference of Party veterans: 'We have
not been vigorous enough ... we not infrequently resort to half measures
and have been unable to overcome accumulated inertia. We must now
make up for what we have lost ... We have reached the stage where we
need to turn our entire huge economy into an uninterruptedly
functioning, well-adjusted mechanism'.

Ominously, a few days after this speech, the head of *Gosplan*, in charge for 20 years, told Andropov that any economic experiments must be conducted 'cautiously'. Andropov was thus encountering the entrenched opposition which faced any would-be reformer in the post-Stalinist USSR.

Andropov's economic reforms were a mixture of reasoned measures, influenced particularly by the Hungarian experience, and domestic appeals for harder work. In January 1984 he began a 'limited industrial experiment', modelled partly on Kosygin's measures of 1965. In sectors covered by five industrial ministries, factory managers were given more powers over decision-making, including decisions over production and use of profits. Any surplus manpower created as a result of changes would be reabsorbed elsewhere. Wages and bonuses were more closely linked to production and sales. Central-planning mechanisms remained in place.

These reforms were limited in scope. Andropov was in power for only a few months, and his poor health slowed the pace of reform, in addition to the opposition and apathy which he encountered. Therefore it is difficult to assess the full significance of his economic reforms. However, almost certainly, by only tinkering with the old Stalinist economic system, they would not have put right the underlying problems. Nevertheless, Andropov's reforms were to provide the basis for Gorbachev's early reform experiments in the mid-1980s, and Andropov did at least begin the process of trying to bring the USSR into line with other developing economic powers. Yet Andropov also made a conscious decision to reject Khrushchev's optimism of 1961. Writing in *Kommunist* in 1983, he declared that the USSR was only at the beginning of a stage of 'Developed Socialism'. Realism was now coming to the fore.

Andropov made a number of personnel changes lower down the hierarchy to help implement his reform programme. During his 15 months in office, he replaced one-fifth of the Regional Party secretaries (including 9 out of 25 in the Ukraine, and 7 out of 20 in Kazakhstan, one of Brezhnev's power bases), one-fifth of the ministers, and one-third of the departmental heads of the Central Committee Secretariat. Several of Brezhnev's associates were shot for corruption, including the owner of the delicatessen which supplied the Brezhnev household. The wife of one of the sacked ministers reputedly wounded Andropov in an assassination attempt in March 1983.

Despite the changes, Andropov generally maintained orthodox attitudes in one particular respect. Although he told the Soviet people that they should not be afraid of learning from beyond their borders, there were strict limits to freedom of opinion at home. His attitude towards expressions of discontent or dissidence was orthodox. He wanted to clean up the system, not to overturn it. When a group of young Communist intellectuals labelled the 'Russian New Left' argued that the 1917 Revolution had simply led to the emergence of a new ruling class, some of them were arrested. A meeting of the Central Committee in June 1983 discussed 'alien' and 'decadent' trends in the arts. Sakharov and his wife continued to be harassed, and the dissident writer Roy Medvedev was warned to cease his 'anti-Soviet activities'. Jewish emigration was halted, and direct-dialling facilities between the USSR and the outside world were stopped. But even in this area there were some reforms: ordinary citizens were encouraged to voice their complaints to officials, and minutes of important Party meetings were published for the first time, a practice to be continued by Gorbachev.

Andropov's attitude towards outbreaks of nationalist discontent was also cool. He continued the Brezhnev policy of asserting that the objective of Soviet policy was to 'fuse' the different national groups into one Soviet people. He did, however, admit that there had been 'mistakes' in the previous policy towards the nationalities, and he emphasised that economic reforms should benefit all the Soviet nationalities, not just the Russians.

4 Cold War Tensions: 'We are not a Naïve People'

Although Andropov launched some initiatives in foreign affairs, on taking office his attitude towards the capitalist West seemed ambiguous and it was difficult at first to determine whether the transition from Brezhnev would have a positive or a negative effect on Soviet-Western relations. Both he and Foreign Minister Gromyko maintained a firm line towards the West, but they also dropped hints that they wanted better relations. Andropov's first major speech as leader in November 1982 called for a fresh impetus towards arms control, although he made it clear that the USSR would not disarm unilaterally: sending a signal to the West, he declared 'We are not a naïve people'. East-West relationships did not improve significantly. Andropov's continuing attacks upon Reagan's 'Star Wars' policy, and the mutual expulsion of diplomats by Moscow and London, did not help matters. Nor did the offer of an olive branch towards China materially improve Sino-Soviet relations. The Afghanistan War remained a running sore.

During 1983 Andropov launched a new arms-control proposal. He offered a moratorium on the building of anti-satellite weapons if the United States would reciprocate. He also offered to reduce the number of Soviet SS-20 missiles as part of an arms-control agreement with the West, but only if British and French weapons were included in the equation. NATO continued to deploy cruise and Pershing 2 missiles in Europe, and so agreement was not reached. Relations were also soured by the American invasion of Grenada in October 1983. Andropov himself blundered in his dealings with West Germany. In September 1983 he sent Gromyko there to support publicly Helmut Kohl's more left-wing Social Democratic opponent in the German elections. This blatant inter-

Soviet cartoon, 'America' - 1983

ference only boosted Kohl's vote to become German chancellor.

One incident more than any other was to heighten the Cold War tensions. At the end of August 1983 Korean Airlines passenger plane KAL 007 was shot down by Soviet fighter planes near the Soviet Far East coast; 269 passengers were killed, including several Americans. The plane was en route from New York to Seoul, but was 700 kilometres off course and flying in Soviet airspace over a sensitive area. Rumours spread that the plane was on a spying mission. However, the Soviet action initiated an international outcry.

Andropov was on holiday when the crisis broke, recuperating from illness. However, although the decision to shoot down the plane had been taken at the local military level, in accordance with the prescribed procedure, the ultimate responsibility lay with Andropov and Defence Minister Ustinov.

Andropov handled the crisis badly. He was still ill, and there were tensions between the political and military leaders. The Kremlin dithered, first denying knowledge of the incident, then refusing to admit having destroyed the plane, and then finally admitting it, but emphasising that the plane had ignored warnings to turn back. The Kremlin emerged from the affair with a tarnished reputation. There were rumours that the military had caused the incident in order to sabotage Andropov's planned talks on arms control. In any event, it was probably a contributory factor in the breakdown of the Geneva talks, announced by Andropov at the end of November, although the stated reason was the deployment of American missiles in Europe. Brezhnev's policy of détente seemed to be in tatters, and Andropov had not made a positive contribution to Soviet foreign policy.

5 The Triumph of the Old Guard: The Rise of Chernenko

Andropov failed to appear for the traditional Red Square parade in November 1983, although his portrait was carried on floats in the traditional manner. There was a statement that he had a 'cold', but in reality he had serious heart and kidney complaints. From his hospital bed, Andropov continued a reform programme: in December he made renewed calls to the Soviet people for hard work. He also made further changes at the top, removing more Brezhnevite officials. But time was short: Andropov entered a coma and died a few days later, on 11 February 1983.

Andropov had been a private person, but had nevertheless impressed many Soviets and foreigners by the way in which he had refused to develop a personality cult and had insisted upon reform. He had been more aware than other post-war Soviet leaders of the true state of affairs in the USSR and, ignoring the dictates of propaganda, had made a serious attempt to change things. In 1982, on becoming leader, his doctors had given him five years to live; he himself had told a colleague that he would need ten years to carry out a reform programme. Andropov died before much could be changed, and the obstructionism which hindered all Soviet reformers might well have defeated him, even had he lived longer. Nevertheless, Andropov had performed two vital services: he had given hope to those people in the USSR who wanted change, and he had begun the programme of reform principally by promoting men such as Gorbachev and Ryzhkov who were to be the nucleus of the next generation of reformers, and who had more time than Andropov to attempt to realise their plans.

The rumour mill had already been hard at work before Andropov's death. In the autumn of 1983, various names were talked about as Andropov's possible successor. One was Ligachev, while Gorbachev and Romanov were canvassed as the representatives of the younger political generation. Privately, some Soviet officials claimed that Andropov had nominated Gorbachev as his successor, and pointed out in support of this claim that Gorbachev had helped to manage the internal Party elections late in 1983, following which 20 per cent of Party secretaries had been replaced. Gorbachev was already a powerful figure. However, the Brezhnevites were still powerful enough to be able to stake their own claim, and their contender for the leadership was Konstantin Chernenko.

Gorbachev accepted the situation, possibly content to wait, since as the youngest contender he had time on his side. He was even prepared to form a temporary alliance with his rival Romanov, a man of very different temperament. Romanov had been the Party boss in Leningrad for 13 years, and had made the city a supposed model of labour productivity. He himself had been a protégé of Kosygin and Suslov: the latter had promoted him as a hard-liner who would resist détente and refuse concessions to the West. However, Gorbachev was probably in a stronger position than Romanov, and he may even have agreed to Chernenko's promotion in return for a promise that he himself would be the eventual successor.

Chernenko's election as general secretary was contested, but he won. His tenure of office was to be too short to have a really significant impact upon events, and reform-minded politicians marked time. Chernenko was certainly not an obvious choice: at 72, he was the oldest man ever to have become leader. Apart from his obvious lack of charisma, his career had been in the bureaucracy, with no practical experience of key areas such as industry and agriculture. There were certainly many in the Party who doubted his credentials, but they could comfort themselves with the knowledge that since he was old and in ill health, Chernenko was unlikely to last long. In the meantime, as a confirmed Brezhnevite, he would represent the cautious, conservative approach for which many Party loyalists still longed.

Chernenko was a classic example of a Soviet bureaucrat who lacked much intellectual spark or originality, but who rose to prominence through hard work and an ability to manipulate the Party organisation, although he did not have a particularly strong base within the Party himself. At a time when there was a battle for supremacy between conservatives and reformers, he was pushed to the forefront as a representative, if not a coherent mouthpiece, of the former.

The new leader was born in 1911 in a Siberian village. During the 1930s he served as a border guard in Kazakhstan, on the Chinese border, and became a Regional Party secretary in Krasnoyarsk. During the Great Terror of 1937 he was deputy personnel chief of the local NKVD (secret police) in Dnepropetrovsk. During this time he began his long association with Brezhnev. It was not a distinguished record, and later the Soviet propaganda machine had difficulty in glamorising Chernenko's wartime exploits, which comprised the supervision of evacuees and labour camps in Siberia.

Chernenko was transferred to Moldavia in 1948. Brezhnev made him head of propaganda in that republic. When Brezhnev went to Moscow in 1956, he took Chernenko with him to work in the propaganda section of the Central Committee. Thereafter he ran Brezhnev's private office, and in Brezhnev's later years in power, Chernenko became his minder. He even accompanied Brezhnev on holiday and indulged in drinking bouts with his friend. The closeness and the nature of their relationship was summed up in a Soviet joke: 'Brezhnev has been dead for quite some time, but Chernenko hasn't told him'. Chernenko had genuine affection for his master. This was reciprocated, and Chernenko was always at Brezhnev's side. Because of the role that he had played, most Party officials and commentators viewed Chernenko as a useful administrator and personal aide, but not as a politician to be taken too seriously in his own right. But it was precisely these qualities which made him an acceptable figurehead to the old guard, particularly when it was known that he had Brezhnev's personal stamp of approval.

Chernenko's handicaps as leader were evident from the start. He suffered from emphysema, a lung disease with complications of the heart. Often short of breath, he struggled and lost his place during his speech at Andropov's funeral. A Soviet joke at the time of his accession ran: 'Why does Chernenko have three microphones in front of him when he makes a speech? Two of them supply him with oxygen'. Although he did his best to live up to a projected image, visiting factories and making public appearances, Soviets joked that 'You can't have a personality cult without a personality'. Chernenko contrasted poorly with both the intellectual Andropov, whose memory was kept alive by his supporters, and with Gorbachev, whose confident appearances on television contrasted markedly with those of the stumbling general secretary, who was frequently inaudible and furthermore often missed out whole sections of his prepared speeches.

6 Chernenko's USSR: 'Look Before You Leap'

Chernenko set the tone of his secretaryship early on. His acceptance speech to the Central Committee contained an implied criticism of Andropov's reforming zeal: 'It is necessary to evaluate realistically what has been achieved, without exaggerating and also without belittling it. Only this approach prevents mistakes in politics, the temptation to indulge in wishful thinking'. Whilst conceding the need for some economic reform, Chernenko went on: 'We would be well advised to observe in this field the old wives' saying, "Look before you leap"'. His concern for stability was demonstrated by the fact that during his 13 months in office, only four new ministers were appointed, and there were no changes made to the membership of the Politburo, although Marshal Ustinov died in December 1984.

Chernenko's government was a coalition of old Andropov and Brezhnevite supporters. It continued Andropov's drive against corruption, but plans to reduce the size of the bureaucracy were dropped, and Party officials were once again promised jobs for life.

One of Chernenko's first tasks was to preside over the Party Commission investigating a new programme for the Communist Party. Chernenko held to the old opinion that Communism would ultimately triumph over capitalism, albeit by means of peaceful competition, but unlike Khrushchev, he wisely did not offer a precise date, asserting that capitalism still possessed great reserves.

Chernenko showed no signs of having a coherent domestic programme. But he did make a few personal initiatives. One was to emphasise educational advances. In addition, censorship was tightened, and he continued Andropov's hard line against dissidents, while his approach to the nationalities issue was somewhat conciliatory - he emphasised that national concerns should be acknowledged.

In foreign affairs Chernenko demonstrated more energy. He declared that he wanted to restore good relations with the West, and repair the damage done during Andropov's period in office. The USSR, he said, would be 'open to peaceful, mutually beneficial co-operation with all states'. However, it proved difficult to revive détente, particularly as the USA appeared to be linking talks on 'Star Wars' with the issue of the deployment of Soviet missiles in Europe. Nor were relations helped when President Reagan did a 'live' microphone test on American television before a speech, in which he declared that he had signed laws to outlaw Russia, and that the bombing of Russia would begin in five minutes. Relations were also soured by the stepping up of Soviet intervention in Afghanistan, and the Soviet boycott of the Los Angeles Olympics, in retaliation for the American boycott four years before. Détente also faced opposition from powerful pressure groups within the USSR, including the military, which had a low opinion of Chernenko. Nevertheless, Chernenko, who had been associated with Brezhnev's policy of détente, continued to preach peaceful co-existence.

There were signs that Gromyko was operating his own foreign policy. He rudely interrupted Chernenko during meetings with foreign dignitaries in Moscow. This said little for Chernenko's authority, since Gromyko was renowned for being the obedient mouthpiece of others - it was Khrushchev who had said of Gromyko, that if ordered to drop his trousers and sit on a block of ice, he would do so at once and without complaining, and sit there until ordered to stand up again!

In August 1984 it was reported that Chernenko was on holiday. He was actually having medical treatment by the Black Sea, and was taken seriously ill. In his absence from Moscow, Ustinov and Gorbachev ran the government. Gorbachev had already become chairman of the Foreign Affairs Committee of the Soviet Union, and when he was given responsibility for ideology, it was an implicit recognition that he was Chernenko's deputy.

Chernenko was in hospital for two months. Although he appeared briefly in September to greet the return to earth of three cosmonauts, he looked very ill. Inevitably rumours spread, and in the absence of clear direction from the top, a crisis between the military leadership and the politicians developed. Marshal Ogarkov, chief of staff and deputy minister of defence, was sacked. He had been prominent in the aftermath of the Korean Airline affair, and had disagreed with Marshal Ustinov on defence policy. Ogarkov wanted the USSR to concentrate on high-technology, expensive missiles, and had already contradicted the official Kremlin line in 1981 by arguing that the USSR could win a nuclear war. He was probably sacked for being overtly ambitious, and old fears about a 'Bonapartist'-style military takeover of the government had been resurrected.

The arguments between soldiers and politicians had a wider significance. Gorbachev was already talking of the need to spend less on defence and more on consumer goods. His rival, Romanov, supported high levels of defence spending and a hard line against the West. Ogarkov's fall weakened Romanov's position, although it was probably a coincidence that talks on disarmament with the USA finally got under way at this time, albeit in an atmosphere of anti-Reagan propaganda. The prospects for success seemed poor. A 12 per cent increase in the Soviet defence budget was announced, suggesting that the hard-liners still had considerable influence.

Early in 1985 Gromyko announced that it had been agreed that arms-control talks would consider space weapons and strategic and medium-range missiles. However, Chernenko's health was failing fast, and the Politburo was preoccupied with the leadership. Even *Pravda* wrote about the 'problems of the succession', a unique event when the incumbent leader was still alive. One faction within the leadership argued for a youthful, energetic leadership, another for experience. The key factor was the decision of Gromyko to throw his weight behind

Gorbachev. This was important, because Gorbachev's elevation was by no means a foregone conclusion. During the autumn of 1984 Gorbachev had lost his responsibility for agriculture after a series of bad harvests. It was only in November, when his portrait reappeared next to Chernenko's, and it was announced that he would go on a high-profile visit to London, that Kremlin-watchers knew that Gorbachev's star had risen again. This was crucial to the future development of the USSR and of its very structure.

The stroke-ridden Chernenko was kept in the public eye by the Soviet media, whereas Gorbachev was given a low profile. Yet Gorbachev was given great prominence in Soviet information fed to the foreign media. The message was clear: Gorbachev would be the next leader. At home, the Soviets preferred the arrangements for the transition to be finalised in private. This had always been the case in the USSR, except in the case of Stalin, when all the potential successors had been so paralysed with fear of the old tyrant that they had not dared to manoeuvre before his death, even in private.

Chernenko died on 10 March 1985. The political infighting was already virtually over, and Gorbachev's transition to the leadership appeared to be a smooth one. He was supported by the Andropov faction, the KGB, and those parts of the administration that wanted reform. One of the first Gorbachev jokes was to focus on the fact that he was the youngest member of the Politburo: 'What support does Gorbachev have in the Kremlin? None - he walks unaided'.

7 The Rise of Mikhail Gorbachev

By Soviet standards, Gorbachev was not to be in high office for very long, but his tenure was to be of decisive importance for the future of the Soviet people, and for Soviet relations with the outside world.

Gorbachev was born in 1931 at Stavropol in the northern Caucasus, where his grandfather had founded a collective farm. In his school holidays he worked as a combine-harvester operator. He was still in the region when it was occupied by the Nazis during World War II. The two years of occupation, 1942-3, were rather skated over by his biographers. He kept a low profile, whilst some of his compatriots joined the partisans, and others were exiled by Stalin as being 'unreliable'.

In 1950 Gorbachev went to Moscow University to study law. Whilst there he joined the Komsomol and then the Party. Hostile Soviet commentators were to paint an unflattering portrait of him at university, claiming that he supported Stalin's anti-Semitic campaign, calling for Jews to be expelled from the university, and spying on those fellow students he considered 'un-Stalinist'.

Soon Gorbachev began to work his way through a series of provincial Party appointments, from Party functionary in the Stavropol District, to first secretary of the Stavropol Regional Committee in 1970.

Meanwhile, in 1967, he took a second degree in agronomy at the Stavropol Agricultural Institute.

Stavropol was a promising base for an ambitious politician: it was one of the most fertile agricultural regions of the European Soviet Union, and several important Party figures, including Suslov and Andropov, were associated with the region. Gorbachev got to know Andropov well when the latter became a regular visitor to a sanatorium in Stavropol. It was these men who were responsible for promoting Gorbachev to Moscow.

As a rising politician, Gorbachev sailed with the wind. He made steady progress under Stalin, then Khrushchev, then Brezhnev, and finally Andropov. He was younger than most of his colleagues, first as a student Party member, then eventually as a member of the Central Committee, and finally in the Politburo. He was generally regarded as an intelligent, agreeable companion.

Made a Central Committee secretary in 1978, Gorbachev was also given responsibility for agriculture. His political progress now became astonishingly rapid for a Party member in the Brezhnev era. In 1979 he became a candidate or junior member of the Politburo, and a full member in 1980. When Andropov became general secretary, Gorbachev was given responsibility for the economy as a whole, and responsibility for Party personnel. Under Chernenko, with responsibility for ideology, he effectively became the number two.

Gorbachev's rise was due both to his own skill at exploiting the political system, and to the fact that at a time of political flux following Brezhnev's death, he already had older and influential patrons looking for new blood that would address particularly the economic problems facing the USSR. A member of the Central Committee compared Gorbachev favourably with his three predecessors: 'After one leader who was half dead, another who was half alive, and another who could hardly speak, the youthful, energetic Gorbachev was very welcome'.

There was a tendency later, particularly in the West, to depict Gorbachev as a radical reformer from his early days. The reality was that his political apprenticeship was marked by orthodoxy, and had it been otherwise he would not have risen through the system. Gorbachev was not a liberal. He had repeated the official line on most issues, even in the later Brezhnev years - for example, his views on the Afghanistan War and human rights were orthodox - and there is no evidence that his views were substantially different from those of most of his colleagues. However, he did echo Khrushchev and Andropov in his desire to make the system work better. In Stavropol he had learned the virtues of a system of initiative on the collective farms: teams of workers had been paid by results and shared profits. These reforms had been discredited in many people's eyes by a series of bad harvests. But the reforms had been promoted from a desire to catch up with the West economically and technologically, not from a desire to democratise or to introduce capitalism.

The new 54-year-old general secretary told the Central Committee in his acceptance speech that the Soviet Union would only make a 'decisive turn' in economic progress through a 'perfection of the economic system'. This was not the talk of revolution. When he was upbraided in London over the Soviet record on human rights, he retorted, 'You govern your society and leave us to govern ours'. In his funeral speech for Chernenko in Red Square, he declared that the USSR would prevail by 'force of example in all fields of life - economic, political and moral', whilst there must be a crackdown on 'idle talk, swagger and irresponsibility, in fact anything which contradicts Socialist norms'. Some analysts claimed that this was the language of Lenin's New Economic Policy, but it was also the language of cautious change only within carefully defined boundaries. The speeches were made by a man who seemed confident and at ease with people at home and abroad. It is little wonder that the British prime minister, Margaret Thatcher, declared on meeting Gorbachev in London: 'I like Mr Gorbachev. I can do business with him'.

Western commentators were intrigued by the fact that Gorbachev's glamorous wife Raisa went shopping in the West End rather than making the traditional visit to the grave of Karl Marx in London. But if the commentators believed that the new leadership was about to abandon the whole ethos of Soviet Communism, they were deluding themselves, or were succumbing to skilfully projected image-building by the Soviet leadership. Certainly nobody had a clear understanding of Gorbachev's reforming intentions at the time of his accession to the general secretaryship.

Andropov		Chernenko	
Domestic	*Foreign*	*Domestic*	*Foreign*
Conservatism v radicalism	Cold War tensions	Temporary triumph of conservatism	Peaceful co-existence
	Arms control		Resurrection of détente
Efficiency and discipline	KAL 007 incident	Weaknesses as leader	
Economic reforms		Arguments over reforms	
Ideological orthodoxy		Struggle for leadership	

Summary - The Andropov-Chernenko Interregnum, 1982-5

Making notes on '*The Andropov-Chemenko Interregnum, 1982-5*'

This chapter covers a narrow time span, but includes several events of significance. This is because these years marked the end of one era, that of stability under the long-term leadership of Brezhnev. Then, after a period of manoeuvring and transition under two leaders, who now appear almost as stopgaps, there was the beginning of an important period of change under Gorbachev. The three intervening years saw changes in personnel in the Soviet administration, conflicting ideas on whether stability or reform were in the USSR's best interests, and also significant developments in the USSR's relationships with other countries. Decide in particular what was the significance of these years for the future of the Soviet Union. The following headings and subheadings should provide a suitable framework for your notes.

1   The succession to Brezhnev
2   The rise of Yuri Andropov
2.1 The significance of Andropov's career before his accession to the leadership
3   Discipline and reform
3.1 What did Andropov mean by 'efficiency and discipline'?
3.2 The significance of the political changes made by Andropov
3.3 How successful was Andropov's domestic policy?
4   Cold War tensions: 'We are not a naïve people'
4.1 Andropov's attitude towards the West and arms control
4.2 What was the significance of the Korean Airlines affair?
5   The triumph of the old guard: the rise of Chernenko
5.1 An assessment of Andropov's achievements
5.2 The contenders for the leadership
5.3 The reasons for Chernenko's accession to the leadership
6   Chernenko's USSR - 'Look before you leap'
6.1 An assessment of Chernenko's domestic achievements
6.2 Chernenko's foreign policy
6.3 Arguments over policy
7   The rise of Mikhail Gorbachev
7.1 The reasons for Gorbachev's rise to prominence
7.2 Gorbachev's views and attitudes

Source-based questions on 'The Androgov-Chemenko Interregnum, 1982-5'

1 Androgov and Economic Reform
Read carefully Androgov's speech to the Central Committee, on page 57. Answer the following questions.
a) What concerns did Androgov express about the Soviet economy in this speech? (3 marks)
b) Whom did Androgov blame for these problems? (2 marks)
c) What remedies did Androgov propose? (4 marks)
d) Was Androgov's confidence about the support referred to in lines 17-18 justified? (3 marks)
e) What evidence is there of propaganda in this speech? (4 marks)
f) Is this speech useful evidence of Androgov's leadership qualities? Explain your answer. (4 marks)

2 Anti-American Cartoon from 1983
Study carefully the cartoon on page 60, and answer the following questions.
a) What is the message of this cartoon? (4 marks)
b) Comment on the tone of this cartoon. (4 marks)
c) Does the cartoon accurately reflect the attitude of the Androgov administration towards the Americans? (4 marks)
d) What do you think was the purpose of such propaganda? (3 marks)
e) Does the fact that this cartoon is very subjective in its treatment make it valueless as historical evidence? Explain your answer. (5 marks)

CHAPTER 5

Gorbachev: *Glasnost* and *Perestroika*, 1985-90

1 The New Leader

The years 1985-90 saw dramatic changes in economic and political structures within the USSR. A period of both optimism and uncertainty gave way to disillusionment and the unleashing of forces which wittingly or unwittingly brought about the collapse of the Soviet Union and beckoned towards an even more uncertain future.

When he became Soviet leader in 1985, Gorbachev gave clear signals that he recognised the need for significant changes in the USSR, particularly in the stagnating economic system. In that year, according to his later account, he had agreed with his friend and colleague, Eduard Shevardnadze, a future foreign minister, that life 'had all gone rotten'. He went on: 'We began looking for an answer to the question: how should we live? ... And we put forward a simple formula: more democracy, more *glasnost,* more humanity. On the whole, everything must develop so that the person in this society feels like a human being'. What is less certain is whether Gorbachev had any more precise plan in mind other than this praiseworthy but generalised sentiment.

There were to be several radical changes in policy during the next five years. This might suggest that Gorbachev did lack clear, long-term objectives. This is what his critics claimed, particularly conservatives on the right. Gorbachev's supporters were to argue that he was learning from the effects of his policies as he went along, and making sensible adaptations as a result. Many ordinary Soviet citizens were to feel confused and even betrayed, or looked back nostalgically to days of certainty, as the promised better life failed to materialise.

The new leader did eventually outline his vision in more detail, although some of his comments were coloured by hindsight. For example, Gorbachev wrote in *Pravda* in 1989 about the development in his thinking, under the heading 'The Socialist idea and revolutionary *perestroika*'. He stated that initially he had thought that it would suffice to eliminate shortcomings from Soviet life within the existing structure. But he had come to realise that a radical restructuring of society was necessary. In carrying out this restructuring, or *perestroika,* the USSR must avoid the excesses of both the Soviet past and the capitalist West. Russia had chosen the correct path in 1917. However, it should now learn from the experience of other countries and proceed along the road towards 'public, self-managing Socialism', a system in which the state would give up much of its interventionist role.

Unfortunately for Gorbachev, many powerful forces inside the USSR did not share his vision. Conservatives had more veneration for the

Soviet past and believed that the maintenance of discipline and social control was more important than reform. Such people thought that the Communist Party should rule alone, and dismissed multiparty, democratic politics and market-style economic reforms as a recipe for chaos. Although the conservatives had no coherent programme themselves, their sentiments did strike a chord with many ordinary Soviet citizens.

In his early days of power, Gorbachev did not appear particularly radical. He had made his career in the Party and he intended that it should stay in control of the reforming process. However, he was realistic enough to realise that social and economic progress would be unlikely if the Brezhnevite old guard was allowed to monopolise key positions in the government and Party. There had to be major personnel changes. But only towards the end of the decade, when Gorbachev's commitment to radical reform had become more pronounced, the Communist Party was facing competition from other political groupings for the first time, and Article 6 had removed the Party from its 'leading role' in society, did Gorbachev give up his expectation that the Party could earn its right to stay in control of the reform process. Even after the failure of the 1991 coup against him, a coup carried out by Communists, Gorbachev was reluctant to concede that the days of control by the Communists were over. This, more than anything, helps to explain why he was increasingly seen as superfluous by those in the USSR who wished the reform programme to continue. Gorbachev was considered too much a product of the old system to be able to carry the reform programme beyond certain limits.

2 Political Consolidation

Chernenko died on 10 March 1985, but Gorbachev had in effect already been running the USSR for the previous three months. Therefore the transition to the 'official' leadership was made to appear as smooth as possible. Nevertheless, Gorbachev had determined enemies in the Politburo. One was his old rival, Romanov. Another was Victor Grishkin, the 70-year-old Moscow Party boss. To counterbalance them, Gorbachev had powerful allies. One was Gromyko, who nominated Gorbachev as general secretary, praising his 'brilliant analysis and decision-making in both domestic and foreign policy', whilst asserting that 'Mikhail Sergeevich has a nice smile, but he also has iron teeth'.

Like all Soviet leaders, Gorbachev had to consolidate his own position as general secretary by promoting his supporters and removing his enemies at all levels. The days of Stalin's bloody purges were long gone, but Gorbachev's methods of establishing his ascendancy were no less effective for being humane. A purge of the Party involved the holding of local Party meetings at which officials were upbraided for corruption and inefficiency. The changes affected all levels. Several government ministers were replaced by their deputies. Changes were made in the Politburo. Three of Gorbachev's principal supporters were promoted to full Politburo membership in April 1985: Yegor Ligachev, Nikolai Ryzhkov, and Victor Chebrikov, the head of the KGB. Ligachev was given responsibility for ideology, a sign that he was being groomed for the number-two position. However, he would soon be labelled by his leader an 'impediment to reform' and would be removed from the centre of power.

The old guard was weakened by the fall of Romanov at the Central Committee plenum of July 1985. The ground was prepared by a campaign of rumours which emphasised Romanov's supposed incoherence, alcoholism and extravagant lifestyle, in contrast to that of the austere, teetotal Gorbachev. Popular, and probably authentic, stories about Romanov included his borrowing a priceless Catherine the Great-era dinner service from the Leningrad Hermitage for his daughter's wedding reception, following which he smashed the dishes like a peasant. He also created a scandal by entertaining his mistress, a Leningrad pop singer, in a box at the opera reserved for the Politburo.

Romanov's removal was popular in many quarters. More surprising to many was the simultaneous promotion of Eduard Shevardnadze to be in charge of foreign affairs. Gromyko agreed to retire after 30 years in that post, accepting instead the ceremonial title of chairman of the Presidium of the Supreme Soviet. Shevardnadze had made his name in his native Georgia by attacking corruption within the Party there, but he was relatively unknown in Moscow and furthermore had no experience of foreign affairs.

By 1987 Gorbachev had the support of three-quarters of the Politburo. The last Brezhnevite, Shcherbitsky, first secretary of the Ukraine, was removed in 1989. Gorbachev had already announced that the Party leadership and the presidency would no longer be combined. He wanted to concentrate on the Party and the economy.

Other changes were equally significant. New military appointments were designed to strengthen Gorbachev's ties with the services. New diplomatic appointments were made abroad. In September 1985 Ryzhkov became prime minister. At the end of the year Grishkin was replaced as Moscow Party boss by the 50-year-old Boris Yeltsin. Yeltsin had risen rapidly from relative obscurity to become a Central Committee secretary in July 1985. He made a strong attack on corruption in the Moscow Party apparatus, sacking six out of the seven Party secretaries.

The purges continued at various levels. Between 1986 and 1989 all 14 of the Republican first secretaries were replaced, along with two-thirds of all secretaries of regional, territorial and Republican Party organisations, and 70 per cent of Party officials at district and city level. Fifty-two per cent of Gorbachev's Central Committee were new members, many of them relatively inexperienced. By 1991, at the very top, only Gorbachev of all the members of the Politburo had served at that level during Brezhnev's lifetime, and the leadership was generally both younger and better educated than in Brezhnev's day.

Changes in the state apparatus paralleled those made in the Party. Forty-two new ministers were appointed. They were often men who had achieved recognition through their successful management of advanced 'show enterprises'. Prime Minister Ryzhkov was among them, having been the director of a machine-building enterprise in Sverdlovsk.

Political reform was not at the head of Gorbachev's agenda when he came to power. Economic growth was the priority. However, Gorbachev soon realised that one was dependent upon the other, and political reform was to become one of several of his preoccupations from 1987 onwards.

3 Populism and *Glasnost*

Gorbachev's personal style as leader provided a stark contrast to all three of his predecessors. He was confident and self-assured in public, and used this to his advantage early on. An asset was his glamorous wife Raisa, who was often prominently at his side, in contrast to the wives of previous Soviet leaders. Western newspapers tended to focus on Raisa's expensive clothes and the couple's lifestyle, but Gorbachev valued her intelligence, telling the Western press that they discussed most major issues together before he made decisions.

Gorbachev demonstrated the new style early on. Like Khrushchev many years before, he liked to talk to 'ordinary' people. He projected a 'cult of modesty', and it was notable at one Congress that he upbraided a speaker for mentioning his name too often during a speech. In April 1985 Gorbachev took part in his first Western-style walkabout. He visited hospitals, factories and schools, both to hear people's views and to put across a reforming message. A visit to a working-class couple on a housing estate for tea was widely publicised. Such events were carefully stage-managed and given blanket coverage in the media, but Gorbachev was skilful enough to appear relaxed and spontaneous, and his image as a thoughtful, approachable leader blossomed both at home and abroad. Ministers and officials were obliged to follow Gorbachev's lead, often appearing on television and radio to answer consumers' complaints, something unheard of before.

Gorbachev's frankness was a quality which he wished to extend to Soviet life more generally, and indeed he regarded it as a precondition of political and economic reform. He denied that 'Stalinism' was a problem: that was simply 'a notion made up by opponents of Communism and used on a large scale to smear the Soviet Union and Socialism as a whole', (interview with the French Communist paper *L'Humanité* in 1986). Nevertheless, like his mentor, Andropov, before him, Gorbachev spoke of the Brezhnev period as a time of missed opportunities for change, a time when necessary decisions had been put off - a time of 'a curious psychology: how to change things without really changing anything'.

Gorbachev was advocating *glasnost*. This word was often translated in the West as 'openness'. However, in 1985 Gorbachev did not intend the word to be equated with complete freedom, particularly for the media. The Russian word also means 'publicity', and implies a greater willingness to explain the reasoning behind decisions.

Gorbachev had a number of motives for encouraging *glasnost*. First and foremost, he could not begin effective reforms unless there was an unambiguous admission first of all that changes were necessary. He was also convinced that the policy would strengthen his regime, and that it was the sign of a confident, mature people: as *Pravda* declared, 'Timely and frank release of information is evidence of trust in people, respect for their intelligence and feelings, and their ability to assess events'. Openness would also promote awareness of incompetence and corruption, and would assist Gorbachev's attempts to root them out. It was precisely for this reason that conservatives criticised *glasnost* as an invitation to turbulence and social instability.

However the word is translated, *glasnost* got off to a bad start. Details of the Chernobyl nuclear-reactor disaster in the Ukraine in April 1986 were acknowledged in the media only after several days of concerned speculation in the West. Influence was excited at both the central and local levels within the USSR to suppress bad news or criticism, as had always been done. Topics such as environmental pollution and problems in the Soviet space programme were taboo subjects as far as open discussion was concerned. Party officials distrusted what they termed 'sensationalism'.

Nevertheless, many restrictions were lifted, and some sensitive areas were re-examined. At the political level, prominent victims of Stalin's purges, such as Bukharin, were posthumously rehabilitated. In 1987 Gorbachev was still dismissing Trotskyism as 'leftish pseudo-revolutionary rhetoric', but eventually a decree of August 1990 allowed for the rehabilitation of all victims of Soviet political repression that had suffered between the 1920s and 1950s. About one million sentences were reviewed and repealed. In another significant admission of guilt, in 1988 the USSR at last acknowledged the existence of the secret protocols signed with the Nazis in 1939, which had allowed for the Soviet takeover of the Baltic states.

Intellectuals were the most enthusiastic supporters of *glasnost*. This was principally because it now became easier to publish 'controversial' material, as censorship was relaxed after 1986. Publishers were given responsibility for monitoring output, although Party officials still exercised a watchful eye. Some notable works were published in the 1980s for the first time, although many of them had actually been written years before: for example, the novel *Dr Zhivago,* written in the

'*In memory of the Seventeenth Congress of the Communist Party*'

The class Soviet decrees

1950s. Its author, Boris Pasternak, was posthumously restored to the Writers' Union in 1987. Famous victims of political repression such as Sakharov and Osip Mandelstam had their memoirs published. The works of several Russian emigrés were published for the first time, ranging from Nabokov's *Lolita* to Solzhenitsyn's epic works about the Soviet experience under Stalin. Controversial foreign works were also published in the USSR: those of the Marquis de Sade; George Orwell's *1984* (1989); and Hitler's *Mein Kampf.* Films making frank political or social statements were also released.

There were other benefits. Restrictions on emigration were relaxed. Some former emigrés, such as the ballet dancer Mikhail Baryshnikov, returned home. Television became more open and lively. Interviews with Western politicians were shown. The press began to debate previously taboo subjects like suicide, abortion and crime, aberrations scarcely before acknowledged officially within the USSR.

However, although some polls suggested that Soviet citizens believed *glasnost* to be an important part of Gorbachev's reforms, it was less vital to ordinary citizens than to intellectuals. The ordinary citizen was more concerned with the impact of economic reform, or lack of it, on his or her daily life.

Gorbachev initially established a close relationship with the Soviet press, but it then deteriorated under press criticisms to the point where freedom of expression came under a renewed threat. The Press Law of June 1990 abolished censorship in establishing the right of all citizens to have open access to information and freedom of expression, and monopolies within the media were banned. But there was a sting in the tail: all public media had to be registered with the authorities, and there were legal penalties for 'unreal' reporting. The State Radio and Television Committee was reconstituted as a means of exerting government influence after Gorbachev became annoyed at growing criticism of his policies.

Glasnost proved a double-edged weapon for Gorbachev. The rediscovery of the past and the open re-examination of the Stalin period were important in politicising the Soviet people. However, Gorbachev's failure to confine criticism to Stalin and Brezhnev, and the attacks on Lenin's memory by 1989, were an important factor in causing a decline in the legitimacy of the Communist Party.

4 *Perestroika:* Reconstruction and Economic Reform

Previous attempts at economic reform in the USSR had been hampered by a reluctance of bureaucrats and administrators at the middle level to change things, or were sabotaged through outright opposition from those who objected to reform on ideological grounds, or who feared the loss of their own positions or privileges. This happened during the 1970s and early 1980s, and was to continue. Gorbachev introduced *perestroika,* or restructuring. He avoided the word 'reform' at first. He preferred the blander phrase 'improving the economic mechanism'. During his first two years of power, Gorbachev thought in terms of encouraging a more purposeful approach towards making the existing system work better, rather than any fundamental restructuring of the old Stalinist or Brezhnevite economic system. He was continuing where Andropov had left off. The architect of *perestroika* was thought by many to be Alexander Yakolev, one of Gorbachev's advisers.

In February 1985 Gorbachev blamed the economic slowdown on the reluctance of officials to make necessary improvements. The theme was repeated in his report to the Twenty-seventh Congress of the Party in February 1986:

1 Every readjustment of the economic mechanism begins with a rejection of old stereotypes of thought and actions, with a clear understanding of the new tasks. This refers primarily to the activity of our economic personnel, to the functionaries of the central links
5 of administration. Most of them have a clear idea of the Party's initiatives and seek and find the best ways of carrying them out ... It is hard, however, to understand those who follow a 'wait and see' policy, or those who do not actually do anything or change anything. There will be no reconciliation with the stance taken by
10 functionaries of that kind. We will simply have to part ways with them. All the more so do we have to part ways with those who hope that everything will settle down and return to the old lines. That will not happen, comrades!

The solution, Gorbachev thought, lay in giving more initiative to managers at factory level, freeing the central planners in Moscow to focus on strategic planning, and deciding on priorities for investment. There was no intention to abolish central planning or to institute a Western-style market economy. Such a development would have had profound ideological as well as economic implications, and would have challenged the Party's leading role in the economy and society. It was only when Gorbachev's initial attempts to reinvigorate the economy had clearly failed that he began to consider more fundamental reform.

Gorbachev wanted to regroup over 60 industrial ministries and state committees into a maximum of seven 'superministries'. In his first year of office he created three of these: in agriculture, machine-building and energy. Gorbachev was keen to promote investment in agriculture and high-technological engineering: in other words, he recognised the need for improvements in quality as well as quantity if the USSR were to compete with more advanced economies.

Initial plans to promote growth in the economy were ambitious. The Twelfth Five-Year Plan (1986-90) assumed that national income would double by the year 2000. The bulk of new investment was to be directed at European Russia rather than Siberia, an area which had received favourable treatment under Brezhnev.

Soviet Economic Growth, 1986-91						
(% figures, from official Soviet sources)						
	1986-90	1986	1987	1988	1989	1990
National income produced	4.2	2.3	1.6	4.4	2.4	-4.0
Industrial output	4.6	4.4	3.8	3.9	1.7	-1.2
Agricultural output	2.7	5.3	-0.6	1.7	1.3	-2.3

The targets could not be met. The annual rate of growth between 1986 and 1989 was a modest 3.7 per cent, a percentage not noticeably different from that achieved in the last years of Brezhnev and his successors. The reality of the plan was that much of the new investment went into energy and agriculture, but relatively little into machine-building, as had been intended, because those former sectors of the economy were controlled by large and powerful ministries which used their influence to obtain favourable treatment.

1980s poster: 'No admittance! In the factory and works, mortal battle is declared against drunkenness'

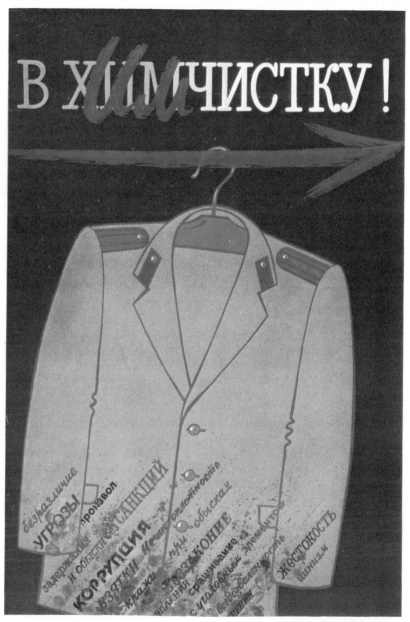

1988 poster: 'In need of a clean!' The policeman's uniform is stained by words such as 'arbitrariness', 'corruption', 'lawlessness', and 'cruelty'

Gorbachev recognised the problems early on, and more radical measures were attempted following the Twenty-seventh Party Congress of February 1986. Gorbachev told the Congress that economic growth was 'the key to all our problems, immediate and long term, economic and social, political and ideological, domestic and foreign'. In 1987 factory managers and farm directors were given a say in what to produce and whom to employ, rather than these decisions being taken by the central planners. Self-financing was phased in between 1987 and 1989: enterprises were to pay for operating costs out of their own profits. A quality inspection agency was created in 1987 to enforce higher standards. A law of January 1987 increased the scope of private economic activity: privately owned businesses and co-operatives were permitted, although they were hedged around with restrictions. Farmers were now to be allowed to lease land from the state and to work it for their own benefit.

The results of these efforts to boost an ailing economy were disappointing. This was particularly so in agriculture, but in 1990 and 1991 industrial production also suffered, actually declining. The Soviet economy was simply not capable of achieving higher growth rates *and* qualitative improvements simultaneously, particularly when many of those in key positions applied the reforms half-heartedly.

Gorbachev and the reformers tried to use Lenin to legitimise the changes taking place: *perestroika* was linked to the NEP of the 1920s; *glasnost* was linked to the soviet movement in the immediate post-revolutionary years; and it was claimed, unconvincingly, that had Lenin lived longer, he would have legalised political opponents and introduced a multiparty system.

Gorbachev was commenting on the problems as early as 1988:

1 We have got to be self-critical; we must see clearly that despite all the positive effects, the state of affairs in the economy is changing too slowly. Some advances are on hand. But they cannot satisfy us. In substance, the increase we have achieved in food output has
5 largely been used to cover the demand connected with the growth of the population ... And those who are holding up the process, who are creating hindrances, have got to be put out of the way. Difficulties arose largely due to the tenacity of managerial stereotypes, to a striving to conserve familiar command methods
10 of economic management, to the resistance of a part of the managerial cadre. Indeed, we are running into undisguised attempts at perverting the essence of the reform, at filling the new managerial forms with the old content. And what is most intolerable is that enterprises are being compelled by means of
15 state orders to manufacture goods that are not in demand, compelled for the simple reason that they want to attain the notorious 'gross output' targets ... Enterprises that have been

given the right to reward their more efficient workers and cut down
on the incomes of those who are lazy, wasteful or idle, are using it
20 much too timidly in fear of offending anyone. To put it plainly, the
reform will not work, will not yield the results we expect, if it does
not affect the personal interests of literally every person.
Address to the Special Nineteenth Party Conference in Moscow,
June 1988.

But many Soviet citizens in all walks of life were uneasy about these
developments. After all, the official line of Marxism-Leninism had
always been that state control was essential for the well-being of the
people. Private enterprise was held to encourage selfish individualism
and to widen the gaps between classes. For this reason, Gorbachev did
not envisage privatising heavy industry, transport or the public services -
what Lenin had called 'the commanding heights of the economy'.
Unconvincing attempts were made to portray Gorbachev's economic
reforms as being in the mould of Lenin's NEP, a period which had
aroused similar ideological concern among many committed Communists. The confusion in many Soviet minds was illustrated by a Soviet joke
popular in 1990:

1 Gorbachev tells the Congress that he wants to change the seating.
    'Let all those who want capitalism sit on the right, the rest on the
  left.' After everyone else has taken their new places, one deputy is
  still hesitating. Gorbachev asks him what the matter is.
5   'I believe in Socialism but I want to live under capitalism', the
  unhappy deputy replies. 'Come up on to the platform then',
  responds Gorbachev.

The tide of reform continued. A vigorous campaign was launched
against the black market, although it actually helped the Soviet economy
to function by filling gaps for which the official outlets could not
provide. Laws in 1987 and 1988 permitted foreign businesses to own
capital assets in the USSR for the first time since 1917. In 1988
collective farms were given more autonomy, and their workers were
given the same rights to elect managers as their industrial colleagues had
been granted.

Many Soviet citizens did not benefit directly from these decrees.
Enterprises which were now responsible for their profitability were less
keen than before to keep on surplus workers. Unemployment became a
major issue in the USSR for the first time. Also, the material benefits
expected under *perestroika* did not come about. Although the quality of
some goods did improve, the overall efficiency and competitiveness of
Soviet produce continued to decline. The private sector of the economy
remained small. This was scarcely surprising, since the directors of
powerful state enterprises used their influence to protect their own

domains, for example, by ensuring that the centralised supply system restricted supplies to private concerns.

Opposition to Gorbachev's *perestroika* came not only from old-style Communists and bureaucrats, and from ordinary people afraid of the future, but from some distinguished intellectuals. Gavril Popov, a professor of management at Moscow University, was a leading spokesman of the radical opposition in the mid-1980s. He characterised the Soviet economy as 'bureaucratic socialism', which discouraged innovation and initiative, and which promised the people material welfare without giving them a real say in their own destinies. Popov declared that Gorbachev was relying too much upon change from above, and claimed that this approach simply strengthened the existing system. The logic of Popov's argument was the opposite to Gorbachev's: he believed that political reform should be the first priority, since genuine and lasting economic reform could only take place in a democratic society. Some other economists also disagreed with Gorbachev's approach. Several of them issued their own reform programme in November 1986, advocating even more self-determination for financial enterprises.

By 1989 it was possible to identify three broad strands of economic thinking in the USSR. The 'old school', sometimes termed the 'Slavophile tendency', harked back to the certainties of the previous decade, and wanted nothing to do with a market economy and its associated features of risk, private property and unemployment. Such believers stressed the importance of stable prices and collectivism. In contrast, the radical Socialists, who included many economists in their ranks, wanted self-management of business, coupled with incentives for workers. However, these advocates also wanted to preserve the 'Socialist' character of the economy by insisting that workers in agriculture and industry should lease enterprises from the state rather than own them outright. Gorbachev and his advisers inclined towards this view by the late 1980s. There was a third, and even more radical, tendency, sometimes called the 'Westernising' or liberal tendency. Its proponents argued that a market economy was essential in a modern, interdependent world: free markets and a strong international currency were the only possibilities, even if such a strategy ran the risk of unemployment. This approach was too radical for Gorbachev. He did change his stance on economic reform as the nature of the problems became more evident, but this was seen by most Soviets not as a sign of the flexibility of a skilful leader, but as the floundering of a politician who had embarked upon a programme of reform without a clear idea of its goals and grand strategy. He was surrounded by conflicting advice. A Soviet joke of 1990 had Gorbachev declaring: 'President Mitterand of France has 100 lovers. One of them has AIDS. He doesn't know which. President Bush of America has 100 bodyguards. One of them is a terrorist. He doesn't know which one. I have 100 economic advisers. I don't know which is the right one'.

5 Party and Politics

One year after Gorbachev came to power, the Twenty-seventh Party Congress was held, in February and March 1986. The 5000 delegates approved the political and administrative changes which had already been made. The Central Committee Secretariat was given a larger role in decision-making. The first woman near the centre of power since Khrushchev's day was promoted: Alexandra Biryukova, who was given responsibility for the supervision of light industry, consumer services and food.

A new Party programme was also ratified. It was the first major modification since Khrushchev's 1961 programme, although Brezhnev and Andropov had both considered changes. Khrushchev's over-optimistic pronouncements about a Soviet Union overflowing with abundance had long been recognised as unrealistic, but now it was publicly stated for the first time that progress towards the classless Communist society would be 'uneven, complex and controversial'. It was still expected that economic progress would be rapid. The Congress implicitly criticised Brezhnev by referring to the 'inertness' and 'self-congratulatory ways of the past'.

A year later, in January 1987, Gorbachev told the plenum of the Central Committee that the Soviet economy and society were in 'crisis', and that the political leadership was 'deaf to social issues'. Therefore the political system must be 'democratised'. There should be genuinely competitive elections for local soviets and Party posts, in order to allow people with genuine zeal access to positions of responsibility, even if they were not members of the Party.

This plenum marked a new stage of political reform. Gorbachev declared, 'A house can be put in order only by a person who feels that he owns this house'. A month later, he told the All Union Council of the Trade Unions that democratic reforms would be 'a guarantee against the repetition of past errors, and consequently a guarantee that the restructuring process is irreversible'. There was no choice: 'either democracy or social inertia and conservatism'.

Gorbachev was still thinking as a Socialist. He emphasised that democratisation would strengthen Socialism. However, at the Nineteenth Party Conference of June-July 1988 he came close for the first time to criticising the 1917 Revolution, or at least its aftermath, which had seen 'serious deformations' leading to repression and a 'command-administrative' rather than a democratic society. All this was a prelude to the setting up of a constitutional review commission and radical political changes. In June 1987 multicandidate elections were introduced into some constituencies, and were then extended to all by the new Electoral Law of December 1988. At the same time, discussions were held to make local soviets genuinely representative, with real power over legislation and local enterprises. Gorbachev proposed a full-time congress of people's deputies, which would elect a smaller, full-time, Supreme Soviet. The latter would supervise the state structure through committees, and would nominate the prime minister.

Elections to the new Congress were held in 1989. It was a complex process, and dominated as they were by the Communist Party, the elections were hardly free. Nevertheless, the elections were a real milestone and a traumatic event for the Soviet people, and represented an important stage on the road to a 'civil society'.

First of all, nominations had to be approved by a territorial constituency or a 'social organisation'. Then the approved candidates competed in the real election. It was hardly a democratic election in the Western sense: 750 seats were reserved for organisations or privileged groups such as the Communist Party, the Komsomol, and the trade unions; 750 seats were reserved for the territorial districts, and 750 for representatives from the nationality areas. The Communist Party was allocated 100 seats and nominated exactly 100 candidates, including most members of the Politburo and the Secretariat, in order to preclude competition within its own ranks.

In the event, about 50 senior regional Party secretaries who did not have 'reserved' seats were defeated in the elections, along with many local government officials and half of the military candidates; 89.8 per cent of eligible voters turned out. This was a lower figure than in the old days, but these were voters who came to the polls of their own free will, not because they were dragooned by state or peer-group pressure. Boris Yeltsin, one of Gorbachev's critics, was not nominated by the Communist Party. He had to undergo a 13-hour selection conference before he was nominated for a Moscow territorial seat. The attempt to humiliate Yeltsin was an important factor in his turning against the Party and his personal rivalry with Gorbachev by 1990.

In all, 2,884 candidates contested 1,500 constituencies. In 384 of them there was only one nominee. Ironically, 87.6 per cent of the new deputies were Communist Party members, a larger percentage than had been elected under the pre-reformed system. Over 65 per cent of the new deputies were 'administrators', and female representation was virtually halved, to 17 per cent.

The nature of the new political order was unclear. Gorbachev was elected to the new post of chairman of the Supreme Soviet in May 1989, and the way was open for further change. The Politburo had already lost much of its influence in policy-making. Now it operated in the public eye, with its agendas published in *Pravda,* so that citizens knew what was being discussed. It now also met monthly rather than weekly. Many of its members who had held both Party and government positions were replaced. These were clear danger signs for the Communist Party. The younger generation was losing its faith. The Komsomol was declining in popularity: its membership fell from 42 million in 1985 to 38 million in 1988, and even the head of the Komsomol could not persuade his son to join it.

By the late 1980s, Gorbachev had consolidated his hold on the higher reaches of the Party, just as the Party's monopoly of power was coming under threat. Power was passing from the Party, and the Politburo in particular, to the presidency and other new institutions. But these institutions did not provide as secure a power base as previous Soviet leaders had enjoyed within the old Communist Party of Brezhnev's day. Gorbachev was therefore unwittingly weakening his own authority within the USSR.

6 Living and Working Conditions

Perestroika was either feared, welcomed, or regarded with indifference. Amongst those who positively welcomed change were large numbers of professional people and intellectuals who believed that reform would generally give them more freeedom. Some national groups in the republics also believed that they would benefit from reforms which would mean them being less dependent on Moscow. Those who opposed *perestroika* included many older members of the Party who believed in the old command economy and carefully ordered society, and benefited from privileges within the system. In addition, both managers and workers in certain occupations, including the military-industrial complex (which contributed up to 70 per cent of national income), stood personally to lose from the new direction which Gorbachev appeared to be taking, and which involved both a restructuring of industry and a scaling-down of the defence programme. Middle-level managers now had more responsibility in their jobs, but this also meant that they were more accountable and ran risks. As for the population as a whole, it had accepted the old system. Even if people did not believe all the propaganda that they had been fed, their basic needs had been met. Food prices were subsidised, everyone had a job, and there were basic social services. People knew what to expect. Now there was no longer a guaranteed existence. There was talk of market economics, but few understood what this meant. People feared unemployment and price rises. Change meant insecurity. Gorbachev told the people that they must participate if *perestroika* were to work, but they preferred to wait and see. The evidence around them by 1990 was of shortages and an uncertain future.

Although the economic condition of many Soviet citizens did not improve during Gorbachev's period in office, there were some benefits. Gorbachev's anti-corruption campaign, launched in 1985 and 1986, emphasised the need for officials to act within the law. Later there were measures to limit the extent to which the Party or government could interfere in the operation of the courts. Under *glasnost,* even the KGB was subject to criticism, and had to justify itself like any other state institution. The new publicly acceptable face of the KGB was emphasised when a 'Miss KGB' competition was held and widely publicised. However, in comparison to the liberal democracies of the West, the rights of the individual were still circumscribed, as had almost always been the case in Russian and Soviet tradition. In his book *Perestroika*, published late in 1987, Gorbachev advocated a rule of law to guarantee civil liberty on the principle that 'Everything which is not prohibited by law is allowed'. A new criminal code, the first for 30 years, reduced the number of crimes for which there was a custodial sentence, and in 1989 an important legal principle was adopted, namely that the accused was presumed innocent until proven guilty. And yet in 1990 Gorbachev was given wide-ranging emergency powers to ban strikes, demonstrations and publications, and even to impose 'temporary presidential rule' over regions or republics. A law was passed in May 1990 allowing for up to six years in prison for publicly insulting the president. Therefore some authoritarian features of government remained, and the contradictions can partly be explained by the fact that reforms were being implemented in a society which had never enjoyed a long spell of liberal or democratic government.

In terms of social benefits, *perestroika* was a mixed blessing. Expectations were raised, often unrealistically. Gorbachev later paid the price for failing to meet those expectations. For example, there were few serious attempts to deal with the housing shortage, an eternal Soviet problem, and although, following a law passed in 1984, an extension of the number of years spent in secondary education from 10 to 11 was phased in, there was also educational chaos. This was particularly the case when History examinations were abolished in 1988, and a government commission had to be set up to write new textbooks that were less constrained in their treatment of the Soviet past.

Inflation and rising prices brought their own hardship to many people. The traditional solace of alcohol was also denied many Soviet citizens, as production and sales of alcohol were severely restricted in 1986. Alcoholism had been a major economic and social problem. However, this measure more than any other increased Gorbachev's unpopularity, whilst the decline in sales reduced government revenue. Improvements in medical care reduced infant mortality by 10 per cent in the late 1980s, but this advance was less publicised than the complaints about restrictions on alcohol.

Like the West, the USSR was experiencing the problems caused by an ageing population and a growing demand for social services. The Soviet economy could afford to bear the cost even less than the West. The problems were complex, but Gorbachev was blamed by many people for their predicament. Gorbachev had the additional difficulty of trying to cope in many cases with a bureaucracy that was slow or reluctant to reform old habits and procedures.

7 A New Soviet State?

As the 1980s drew to a close, how different was the Soviet state from that inherited by Gorbachev some five years before?

Both *glasnost* and *perestroika* had effected considerable changes, but not all had been intended or expected. Much of the initial suspicion had evaporated. In 1985 and 1986 many people prepared in principle to welcome a more open society had been cautious, afraid that reforms might not be genuine, and that the brakes to free expression might be quickly reapplied. By 1990 there was more confidence in *glasnost:* a population which was on the whole well educated was more prepared to speak out and had expectations of a say in its future for the first time. However, Gorbachev had not provided the people with the means to influence their lives. Political reform had been half-hearted. Those without a real stake in the system saw no reason to be enthusiastic about economic reform. The privileged position of the Communist Party had not been significantly undermined, and its members often dominated the new institutions that had emerged. The new political institutions - the Congress of People's Deputies, the Supreme Soviet, and the presidency - were seen to be lacking in effective power and therefore also lacked credibility. In the republics that were more distant from Moscow, especially in Asia, the Communist Party still held considerable power, or else the Republican institutions were flexing their own political muscles and effectively breaking away from the centre, and indeed the whole federal structure. Gorbachev himself only acted to change this structure when he was forced into a corner.

Gorbachev's initial reforms had clearly proved inadequate. He had tinkered with a system which the reformers themselves hoped could be saved. To his credit, he had faced this reality, and, between 1987 and 1989, with the Party still at the helm, had instituted more political and economic changes from above. But by 1990 both Gorbachev and the Party were losing control of the reforming process as the economy began to disintegrate. Gorbachev had changed direction too many times. People felt confused and betrayed. By trying to maintain the essence of a planned society with some of the benefits of a market economy, Gorbachev achieved the worst of both worlds.

In December 1989, the Congress of People's Deputies voted to accept what was known as the Abalkin Programme of economic reform, with the ultimate objective of denationalising state property and progressing towards a market economy. The state would continue to manage raw materials, fuel and defence. This was a radical advance on earlier programmes. But there were conflicts on the horizon: the government's own programme, introduced by Prime Minister Ryzhkov, was more conservative, ruling out large-scale denationalisation or large-scale private production. There was further confusion in 1990 when Shatalin, a member of Gorbachev's Presidential Council, argued for further radical reform based upon a system of private enterprise reinforced by foreign investment, whilst the state sector would be restricted to the infrastructure. Shatalin's plan was rejected by Gorbachev, and this was to mark a shift to the right by him.

All the economic arguments seemed increasingly unreal. Social stability was threatened by rising inflation and shortages of basic goods. The republics were no longer prepared to take orders from Moscow. In Stalin's day, the Soviet population had been told to tighten its belt and make short-term sacrifices for the sake of promised long-term benefits. That message had been reinforced by propaganda and terror. In 1990 the population was not prepared to make the sacrifice, and the regime no longer had the power to coerce it. Ironically, reforms which were designed to dismantle large sectors of state control could only be safely implemented by a strong government, confident in popular support. This situation did not exist in the USSR, and therefore Gorbachev's regime was heading for a crisis.

Gorbachev had consolidated his power in 1985 remarkably quickly, far more quickly than any of his predecessors, including Stalin. But then he raised expectations which he could not meet, and his shifts in policy brought distrust and cynicism. He himself was to admit after 1991 that he had been too slow in the early years to commit himself to radical reform. What he failed to realise was that by stressing the need to change people's attitudes before changing institutions, he was inhibiting the prospect of success. It was powerful institutions like the Party and the bureaucracy which resisted reform, and they had to be changed if economic and social progress were to have a real chance. Gorbachev learned the lesson too late, although it is doubtful whether any one leader could have succeeded, however wise and able. The entrenched bureaucracy, conservative in both its structures and personnel, could only be altered to a limited extent by the efforts of one individual, which is why Gorbachev insisted that there must be a change in attitudes as well as structures if his reforms were to succeed.

Making Notes On '*Gorbachev:* Glasnost *and* Perestroika, *1985-90*'

This chapter contains a lot of information on a short but very important period in Soviet history: from the coming to power of Gorbachev to the period shortly before an attempt to force him from power. Complex political, economic and social developments occurred during these years. Several names are mentioned which you will have come across in previous chapters or will meet again. At the time when this chapter was written, the events described were so recent, and part of your lifetime too, that historians have only just begun to analyse them. It is difficult to gain a perspective, and the reverberations of these events are still being felt, so we cannot estimate their full significance. Nevertheless, an attempt has been made to analyse Gorbachev's thinking and the impact of the changes which he unleashed.

The notes which you make should contain information about the main events in the Soviet Union between 1985 and 1990, and in particular the changes that were made in politics and the economy, why, and with what results. The following headings and subheadings should assist you.

1   The new leader
1.1 What were the arguments for and against change in the USSR in the mid-1980s?
2   Political consolidation
2.1 How did Gorbachev consolidate his political power in 1985-6?
3   Populism and *glasnost*
3.1 What was new about Gorbachev's leadership style, and how effective was it?
3.2 What were the motives for introducing *glasnost?*
3.3 What were the successes and failures of *glasnost?*
4   *Perestroika*
4.1 What were the origins and meaning of *perestroika?*
4.2 How successful was the Twelfth Five-Year Plan?
4.3 How radical were the economic reforms introduced from 1986 onwards, compared to the measures taken before Gorbachev came to power?
4.4 Why was there opposition to *perestroika* in some quarters?
4.5 What were the main arguments concerning economic reform in the USSR in the 1980s?
5   Party and politics
5.1 Summarise the message of the 1986 Party programme
5.2 What were Gorbachev's motives for introducing political reform in 1987?
5.3 What was the nature and significance of the 1989 elections?
6   Living and working conditions
6.1 What were the different attitudes of the Soviet people to various reforms?
6.2 What benefits did the reforms bring, and what disappointments?
7   A new Soviet state?
7.1 How and why did people's attitudes towards Gorbachev and his policies change between 1985 and 1990?
7.2 In what ways was Gorbachev's position becoming insecure by the end of the 1980s?

Answering essay questions on '*Gorbachev:* Glasnost *and* Perestroika, *1985-90*'

Questions on the period after 1982 may be specifically concerned with domestic events, Soviet foreign policy, or general issues which include

1985 Gorbachev comes to power

MAIN FEATURES:

Consolidation   1986, *Glasnost*   1986, *Perestroika*

THE DIFFICULTIES:

Entrenched   Bureaucracy   Uncertainty   Opposition of
attitudes   vested interests

DISENCHANTMENT

Limited effect   Lack of clear   Difficulty of coming to
of reforms   direction   terms with pluralist democracy
Growing spectre of
nationalist
violence

Summary - Gorbachev: Glasnost *and* Perestroika, *1985-90*

---

both aspects. In this chapter, only essays concerned with domestic events in Gorbachev's USSR will be considered. Other questions will be dealt with in Chapters 6 and 7.

Questions on the USSR after 1982 are likely to focus on political and economic changes: the reasons for them, the way in which they were implemented, and their effects in the Soviet Union.

Consider the following questions, which relate to the issues already outlined above.

1   To what extent did Gorbachev's policy of *perestroika* succeed in reforming the Soviet economy?
2   'Too little, too late.' How far is this a valid assessment of Gorbachev's policies within the USSR?
3   To what extent is it true that, in domestic Soviet affairs in the ten years after Brezhnev's death in 1982, the period was one of 'uncertain government and missed opportunities'.

These questions are all examples of the common 'To what extent/how far' type, requiring you to *analyse,* not describe, and to produce supporting evidence to reinforce your arguments. As in earlier chapters, identify the key words in the titles, then decide upon your main line of approach, and plan your introduction, main body, and conclusion to each essay.

To do full justice to these essays, you may also need to consult Chapter 7.

Question 1 has a narrower focus than the others. The key words are 'To what extent', '*perestroika*', 'succeed' and 'reforming the Soviet economy'. As indicated in earlier chapters, it is difficult to consider the success of a policy without considering the motives behind it. In this case, you will also need to analyse the state of the Soviet economy in 1990, and the situation at the time of Gorbachev's resignation.

You should comment upon the underlying problems of the Soviet economy in the early 1980s: stagnation, low growth rates, lack of enterprise, stifling bureaucracy, overcentralisation, obsolescence, and heavy concentration on defence spending and certain sectors of the economy. Decide the extent to which these were symptoms or causes of the problems (they were often both). Then you should consider Gorbachev's motives for reform, and the different stages of *perestroika*.

You may take the line that *perestroika* was a bold gamble that partially succeeded or failed - in which case you should produce some relevant evidence; or you may take the line that the reforms were never fundamental enough, or that the various stages came too late. You will need to consider the reasons: lack of clear, long-term planning; uncertainty; entrenched opposition from vested interests; lack of time, and so on. As so often with this type of question, there is no clear 'right' or 'wrong' answer. What you *must* do is to maintain a logical line of argument, supported by evidence. In your conclusion, you should be able to compare the state of the Soviet economy at the time of Gorbachev leaving office with the time of his accession to power, and make some reasoned judgments on the basis of that.

Question 2 is presented in a different way, but in fact it has many similarities to question 1. The key words this time are the quotation 'Too little, too late', and the phrases 'How far' and 'Gorbachev's policies'. Although the main part of your answer may well include considerable detail on *perestroika* and the economy, since these were probably the key issues, you should also consider other domestic aspects such as *glasnost* and political reform. Your approach is likely to be similar to that employed with question 1: an assessment of the general state of the USSR in 1985, and then again at the time of Gorbachev's resignation. Good planning of your essay is particularly important to ensure that you have considered all the key areas before you begin. Where possible and relevant you should make links: for example, between *glasnost* and *perestroika*, since Gorbachev himself thought that success in one was dependent upon success in the other. Whether you agree with the quotation or not, refer to it during your essay, partly to ensure that your answer is focused upon the question. As with question 1, consider the reasons why particular policies succeeded or failed, before making your final assessment.

Question 3 is a broader question, which covers the Andropov-Chernenko period as well as the Gorbachev era. The key words are 'uncertain government', 'missed opportunities', 'To what extent' and 'domestic Soviet affairs'. As with question 2, domestic affairs can be taken to include political, economic and social aspects. The main part of your answer is likely to focus upon the Gorbachev period, but do not neglect the previous three years: it should be possible, for example, to make a link between Andropov's promptings of reform and what took place under Gorbachev; you may also feel that the Chernenko period can be used to illustrate the 'missed opportunities' aspect.

'Uncertain government' is a loaded phrase, and you will need to decide how accurate a phrase it is. You might consider changes in *personnel*, but you should also consider *policies*. Did the three leaders between 1982 and 1991 have certain, clear policies, or did these change? You might decide, for example, that although Gorbachev had some clear ideas on reform, his approach to implementing them was uncertain or inconsistent. 'Missed opportunities' could apply to both political and economic reform. You might take the line that some opportunities were grasped, such as *glasnost*, but had only limited success; you might also argue that in promoting a certain pace of economic reform in particular, opportunities were missed.

As with question 2, because this is a broad question with several possibilities, it is particularly important to plan clearly beforehand, so that your essay does not become bogged down in detail, but rather that your line of argument is clear and consistent.

Source-based questions on 'Gorbachev: Glasnost and Perestroika, 1985-90'

1 Gorbachev and Reform

Read carefully the extract from Gorbachev's speech to the Twenty-seventh Congress of the Communist Party in February 1986, on page 78, and answer the following questions.

a) What did Gorbachev mean by 'readjustment of the economic mechanism' in line 1? (4 marks)
b) What sort of people did Gorbachev have in mind when he referred to those who followed a 'wait and see' policy (line 8)? (4 marks)
c) What changes in the Soviet economic system was Gorbachev about to implement at the time of this speech? (6 marks)
d) How reliable is this source as evidence of Gorbachev's determination to reform the Soviet economy in the mid-1980s? (6 marks)

2 Problems in Gorbachev's USSR

Read carefully the extract from Gorbachev's speech to the Nineteenth Party Conference of June 1988 on pages 81-2, and look at the statistical table on the Twelfth Five-Year Plan on page 79, and answer the following questions.

a) What is meant by the word *perestroika*? (3 marks)
b) (i) What benefits does Gorbachev claim to have been the result of *perestroika*? (ii) What problems does he claim had not been solved by it? (5 marks)

c) What, according to Gorbachev, was essential for reform in the USSR to succeed? (3 marks)

d) Contrast the tone and content of this speech with that in source 1. How do you account for any similarities or differences between the two speeches? (4 marks)

e) In what ways are this source and the statistical table valuable to historians studying the difficulties of achieving meaningful reform in the Soviet Union in the 1980s? (5 marks)

3 Anti-drunkenness and Anti-corruption Posters

Study the posters on pages 79-80 and answer the following questions.

a) Outline the messages of these visual sources. (6 marks)

b) How accurately do these sources reflect the changes in official attitudes which were taking place in Gorbachev's USSR? (6 marks)

c) Are these sources more or less propagandist than the examples of Soviet propaganda seen earlier in this book? Explain your answer with reference to the sources. (8 marks)

CHAPTER 6

'New Thinking': Foreign Policy under Gorbachev

1 The Position in 1985

Gorbachev inherited a difficult situation in 1985 with regard to Soviet foreign policy. Détente seemed a distant memory, and the USSR was investing a far higher proportion of its resources than the USA in its attempt to maintain its superpower status and its world-wide influence. The most obvious problem was Afghanistan: here the war was costing a vast amount in men and resources, and apparently the Soviets were no nearer victory after four-and-a-half years of fighting. There were other reminders of the distrust and ill will that permeated international relations: the American failure to ratify the SALT II Treaty and the continued publicity given to President Reagan's 'Star Wars' policy; the deployment of NATO cruise missiles in Western Europe and Soviet missiles near the USSR's borders; and continued foreign criticism of Soviet policy on human rights and Jewish emigration.

Nor had the Soviet Union been notably successful in maintaining its influence in the Communist world. The Communist regimes of Eastern Europe were still tied to the USSR, but they exhibited many of the economic and social problems of their ally and mentor, and they were a drain on Soviet resources such as gas and oil. Although the Solidarity movement had popular support in Poland, the Communist regimes in the Warsaw Pact countries lacked widespread popular support, although they seemed relatively secure.

Relations with China remained a festering sore, as they had done since Khrushchev's day. It was not just an issue of Soviet humiliation at being challenged by China for leadership of the Communist world: a massive 25 per cent of Soviet defence spending went on maintaining forces on the uneasy Chinese border. At the same time, the USSR was getting little obvious return, either moral or practical, from its continuing support of national liberation movements in Africa and Central America.

Therefore the crucial question facing Gorbachev was: should he continue with a 'traditional' Soviet foreign policy, based upon peaceful coexistence, whilst maintaining massive conventional and nuclear forces, and seeking to extend Soviet influence throughout the world? Or should he implement a new policy, taking more account of problems at home, and more in keeping with his reforming domestic policy?

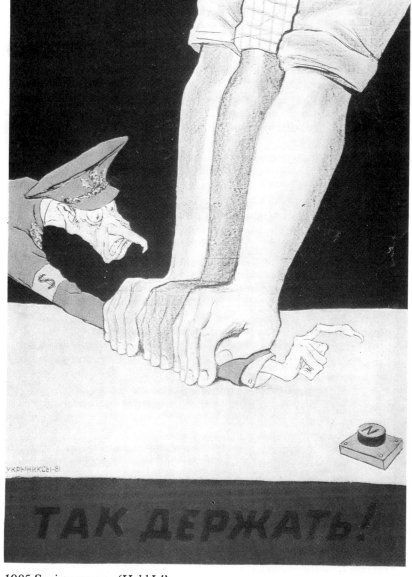

1985 Soviet cartoon - 'Hold It!'

2 'New Thinking'

Gorbachev's views on Soviet foreign policy in 1985 seemed orthodox on the surface, and he was openly critical of what he termed the 'aggression' and 'state terrorism' of the NATO countries. However, he had political and other motives for wishing to reduce international tension and improve the Soviet international standing. He was more aware than most of the strains which the Cold War exerted on the ailing Soviet economy. There was little prospect of successful economic reform without a considerable reduction in defence expenditure. A new foreign policy and *perestroika* were inextricably linked. However, change was potentially difficult: not only did Gorbachev have to overcome traditional distrust of Soviet intentions abroad, but he was also taking on powerful pressure groups within the USSR, including the military establishment and an industrial-scientific complex geared to the expectations of the Cold War, and used to creaming off the best of Soviet technology and resources, whatever the cost.

Gorbachev launched a series of foreign-policy initiatives with a public statement that the world was increasingly interdependent, and that the language of confrontation was both redundant and dangerous. This was the 'New Thinking' unveiled at the Twenty-seventh Party Congress in 1986. The ideas were not new. Some of the implications had already been discussed by Soviet specialists in foreign affairs. But now they were in the open. Gorbachev told the delegates:

1 A turning point has arisen not only in internal but also in
  external affairs. The changes in the development of the
  contemporary world are so profound and significant that they
  require a rethinking and comprehensive analysis of all its
5 factors. The situation of nuclear confrontation calls for new
  approaches, methods, and forms of relations between different
  social systems, states and regions.

At the same Congress he declared:

1 The course of history, of social progress, requires ever more
  insistently that there should be constructive and creative
  interaction between states and peoples on the scale of the entire
  world ... Such interaction is essential in order to prevent nuclear
5 catastrophe, in order that civilisation should survive ... and that
  other world-wide problems that are growing more acute should
  also be resolved jointly in the interests of all concerned ... The
  prevailing dialectics of present-day development consist of a
  combination of competition between the two systems and a
10 growing tendency towards interdependence of the countries of the

world community. This is precisely the way, through the struggle of opposites, through arduous effort, groping in the dark as it were, that the controversial but interdependent and in many ways integral world is taking shape.

The first open criticisms of Brezhnev's foreign policy soon followed. The Central Committee issued a statement referring to the 'dogmatism' and 'subjectivism' of the past, and the fact that Soviet thinking had not kept pace with the realities of world affairs. 'New Thinking' called for radical progress, including the elimination of all nuclear weapons by the year 2000, in a world protected by a multinational and comprehensive security system.

Gorbachev continued to spell out the implications of 'New Thinking'. There was a distinct shift away from the notion that Soviet foreign policy should be based upon the assumption that the world was divided into opposing political, social and economic systems. Gorbachev went much further than Khrushchev and Brezhnev and their ideas of peaceful coexistence. Their thinking had been based on the assumption that, whilst war between the Communist and non-Communist worlds was not necessarily inevitable, Communism would nevertheless eventually triumph by virtue of its superior example. Gorbachev declared that the notion of a foreign policy linked to assumptions about class systems was obsolete.

This was too much for those colleagues still steeped in orthodox Marxist thinking. Yegor Ligachev openly challenged Gorbachev's views in August 1988, declaring that the basis of Soviet foreign policy should remain the 'class character of international relations'. This disagreement was one reason why Ligachev's responsibility for ideology was exchanged for agriculture.

Gorbachev continued to call for more genuine international co-operation to deal with global issues. He promised that the USSR would play a more prominent role in the United Nations, rather than conduct all its foreign policy through bilateral relationships with individual states. He told the UN General Assembly in December 1988 that the UN should play a bigger role in world affairs. He also talked about issues such as pollution and the depletion of natural resources, issues about which the USSR had been noticeably reticent in the past.

'New Thinking' also embraced other aspects of internationalism. Gorbachev insisted that the USSR was not an isolated Socialist economy, but that it was an integral part of the world economy. He advocated the reduction of trade barriers. The USSR began to attend meetings of GATT (the General Agreement on Tariffs and Trade) as an observer, and it applied to join the IMF (the International Monetary Fund). Gorbachev also called for a policy of nuclear disarmament in place of nuclear deterrence, and this policy was written into the 1986 Party programme. 'Equal security for all' became a new catch phrase.

Gorbachev also promised to promote human rights at home and abroad. He convened a human-rights conference in Moscow in February 1987, a conference which Sakharov attended.

'New Thinking' also stipulated that the USSR no longer advocated the exporting of Communism through the encouragement of revolutionary movements in other countries. This was a radical reversal of previous Soviet policy, which from the earliest days of the Soviet Union had been to give material and moral support to left-wing movements in capitalist states. This had always been one of the principal causes of Western suspicion of the USSR. Gorbachev also called for better relations within 'the great Socialist community' itself, including China.

Closer to home, Gorbachev explicitly rejected the Brezhnev Doctrine by declaring that Socialism 'must proceed at its own pace'. In other words, the USSR would no longer automatically reserve for itself the right to interfere in the affairs of the Communist states of Eastern Europe. This was to have important consequences for those states at the end of the 1980s.

Positive pronouncements on foreign relations had been made before, and had been greeted with scepticism by foreign governments. But there was now more willingness to take what was being said seriously, and Gorbachev's reputation abroad blossomed, certainly far more than it did at home.

3 Arms Control and Disarmament

Gorbachev inherited from his predecessors the thorny issue of trying to resurrect arms-control negotiations with the West. In November 1983 the USA had deployed more missiles in Europe, and in response the USSR had walked out of the Geneva Arms Talks then in progress. One unresolved issue was whether, as Gorbachev wanted, British and French nuclear weapons should be included in negotiations.

In November 1985 Gorbachev and Reagan had their much-publicised 'fireside chat'. Gorbachev offered to reduce the number of medium-range missiles and balance them against American, British and French ones. But Gorbachev left Geneva with nothing, because Reagan would not give an undertaking to abandon his strategic defence initiative (SDI), which involved plans to use sophisticated weapons technology in space to counter any Soviet missile threat.

Gorbachev continued to pursue an agreement with the West. In January 1986 he announced a reduction in strategic and intermediate-range missiles, telling the American *Time* magazine that this was necessary if his reform programme at home were to succeed. In September NATO and the Warsaw Pact signed a preparatory treaty on conventional disarmament.

There was a growing mood of optimism. Both East and West made concessions. At the Stockholm Conference in September 1986, the

USA and the USSR agreed to reciprocal inspection of their missile sites, and also that they would give each other prior warning of troop manoeuvres. However, at a summit meeting at Reykjavik in Iceland in October, nothing concrete was achieved. Gorbachev proposed a 50 per cent cut in strategic nuclear forces over several years, without including British and French forces in the calculations. Gorbachev won more praise from neutrals than Reagan, but the latter's refusal to contemplate limits on his SDI programme prevented further progress, and this was the most significant result of the summit.

A breakthrough was finally achieved in December 1987 in Washington. This was the third Reagan-Gorbachev summit, and the most significant. This was what Gorbachev hailed as a 'victory for New Thinking', since there was, for the first time, an agreement on disarmament, as opposed to limits on existing stockpiles of nuclear weapons. The dismantling of short-range missiles in Europe began. There was no direct reference to SDI.

The final Reagan-Gorbachev summit was held in Moscow in May and June 1988, with talks on arms control. Further troop reductions were agreed in November 1989. The new realism continued under Reagan's successor, when Gorbachev and President Bush held a summit off the coast of Malta in December 1989. Bilateral treaties followed on trade, energy and cultural matters. Bush and Gorbachev met again in Moscow in July 1991 with even more significant results: both sides agreed to reduce their stocks of weapons by 30 per cent.

Gorbachev succeeded in building better relations with the West partly because he accepted that the USSR had mistakenly allowed itself to respond to American military might by continuously building up its own forces, which had had two effects: firstly, to weaken the Soviet economy; and secondly, to give ammunition to those opponents of the USSR, who painted it in black terms. Gorbachev's policies also bore fruit because both superpowers were beginning to see Central Europe as less and less vital to themselves in terms of defence, and were therefore more prepared to countenance reductions in their forces and military arsenals there. Gorbachev's own negotiating skills and the generally positive profile he enjoyed in the West were also advantageous factors in improving relations.

4 Eastern Europe

Gorbachev's impact upon Eastern Europe was as significant as his impact within the USSR. The Communist regimes of the Warsaw Pact countries had been politically, militarily and economically bound to the USSR since the aftermath of World War II, and were seen within the USSR as an integral part of the Soviet security system. However, Gorbachev was more conscious than many of his colleagues that developments in Eastern and Western Europe demanded a fresh approach to foreign policy. In particular, he noted the gradual integration of Western Europe into the European Union, and feared that the growth of a powerful Western European bloc might make Eastern Europe more vulnerable. He hoped for a less divided Europe, and so he called for the creation of a 'common European home'.

In 1986 and 1987, in an unprecedented move, Gorbachev travelled throughout Eastern Europe preaching the benefits of economic and political reform. He virtually appealed to the people over the heads of their politicians, and in so doing he undermined the position of old-style Stalinist leaders, such as Honecker in East Germany, who were unimpressed by what was occurring within the USSR. Their position was further undermined by the revelations which resulted from *glasnost*, as when, for example, the past plotting and dealings of some of the Eastern European leaders were made known. Gorbachev openly welcomed examples of reform, such as when there was a change of leadership in Hungary. He also privately warned the Party leaders of the Warsaw Pact countries in 1986 that they could no longer depend upon Soviet military support to bale them out of a crisis. Discussions followed on how to manage Soviet troop reductions in Eastern Europe.

The year 1989 was crucial. Gorbachev reassured Western leaders, and sent further signals to the people of Eastern Europe, by openly renouncing the Brezhnev Doctrine in a speech to the Council of Europe in Strasbourg in July: 'The philosophy behind the concept of a common European home excludes the likelihood of an armed clash and the very possibility of the use or threat of force, above all military force, by one alliance against another, within alliances, or anywhere else'. This clear declaration was reaffirmed shortly afterwards at the last major Warsaw Pact meeting, held in Budapest. The USSR affirmed the right of members of the Pact to make changes within their own countries 'without outside interference'.

To some extent Gorbachev was bowing to the inevitable, but his commitment to reform and non-interference was genuine, and struck a chord with many people in Eastern Europe. The year 1989 witnessed the overturning of Communist regimes in Czechoslovakia, Hungary, Bulgaria and Romania. The people of these countries protested against their leaders in the capital cities, demanding change and reform, and hailing Gorbachev as a hero. The dismantling of the Berlin Wall was of even greater significance. There were many in the West who had doubted whether the USSR would ever permit a reunification of Germany under a non-Communist regime, given Soviet fear of past German aggression, but Gorbachev gave the event his blessing, and welcomed a 'new world order'.

Gorbachev's reputation abroad as a man of vision was greatly boosted by these events. This was the leader who had secured an extension of the Warsaw Pact Treaty in 1985, but who now appeared to be graciously relinquishing Soviet influence over Eastern Europe and, possibly with it, the Soviet Union's status of a superpower. Such behaviour by a Soviet leader would have been unthinkable a few years before. But Gorbachev's actions were not dictated by idealism alone. It would have been difficult for him to implement reform at home without permitting it abroad, and in any case, any Soviet attempt to halt the process would have been dangerous and expensive. At the very least, it would have launched a new Cold War with the West. It was also possible that the USSR might gain from change in Eastern Europe: for years the Soviets had been supplying raw materials such as natural gas and oil cheaply to the Eastern European regimes, and paying high prices in return for their manufactured goods. A reformed and more prosperous Eastern Europe might actually benefit the USSR economically. This was certainly the opinion of reformers such as Foreign Minister Shevardnadze.

5 Mounting Difficulties

It may also have been that the USSR actually miscalculated the extent of the mood for change in Eastern Europe, and was taken by surprise by what happened. If that was the case, Gorbachev accommodated himself to the changes with remarkable ease. This was not the case with his opponents within the USSR. The Twenty-eighth Congress declared in July 1990 that 'the changes in Eastern Europe are not going to upset our friendly relations with the people. The CPSU is of the opinion that the reforms commencing there and the continuing *perestroika* here in the USSR will provide a natural and more stable basis for voluntary contacts of mutual benefit'. But this statement disguised the extent of the disquiet felt by conservatives. There was a widespread fear amongst them of a possible domino effect: if the Eastern European regimes were overthrown or radically transformed in some way, Soviet republics, particularly the Baltic states, might be encouraged to pursue their own, separatist agenda, with dire consequences for the future of the Union.

Shevardnadze in particular was blamed: he had negotiated the withdrawal of cruise missiles from Western Europe, but he had also presided over the dissolution of Soviet control over Eastern Europe. His comments that he could not imagine Soviet forces intervening in a Warsaw Pact country were held by many to have directly contributed to that process. The old slogans which identified the defence of the USSR with the cause of world Communism were not redundant to those of the old school. Shevardnadze resigned in December 1990. He was particularly concerned at the shift to the right that appeared to be taking place within the USSR. Shevardnadze left office complaining that he had not received the backing from Gorbachev that was his due. He felt personally threatened by the criticism he himself had attracted, and he also criticised Gorbachev for assuming emergency presidential powers. Shevardnadze warned of the danger of dictatorship, and spoke his mind in an article in *Pravda* in June 1990:

1 The policy of using military power to underpin diplomacy always
drove states to political bankruptcy or catastrophe. Great empires
collapsed, while states which have practically no armed forces
flourish ... Foreign policy, like domestic policy, cannot defend and
5 protect the indefensible; situations that contradict generally
accepted views on equality, freedom and people's power, or
developments that go against the natural course of history ... When
we talk about ridding inter-state relations from ideological
confrontation we have in mind the need to liberate foreign policies
10 from deformed ideology, and from ideological extremism ... What
reply is there for those who challenge us to explain why we
permitted changes in Eastern Europe, or why we agreed to
withdraw our troops from there? These critics seem to imply that
we should have used tanks to 'bring about order'. Can anyone
15 seriously believe that the problem can be solved by such methods?
... It is time we understood that neither Socialism, nor friendship,
nor good neighbourliness, nor respect can rely on bayonets, tanks
and bloodshed ... We are supposed to be in an era of *glasnost*.
People criticise the diplomats for unspecified concessions which
20 have allegedly harmed our security. Is it not time to speak about
security more openly? Soviet taxpayers have a right to know what
security they are getting for their money.

The newspaper *Isvestiya* published a perceptive article on 2 January
1991:

1 Why didn't anyone mount the rostrum to share the responsibility
and defend Shevardnadze? If you think about it, the answer is
readily apparent: the president needs the army's support more than
ever before, and he doesn't want to see its patience exhausted.
5 International support is easier to secure than domestic support.

The implication was that Gorbachev had sacrificed his reforming
colleague in order to save his own position.

Gorbachev's own position was certainly under attack. Defence
spending still accounted for approximately 25 per cent of gross national
product in 1990, but attempts to reduce this figure were bound to meet
opposition from the armed-forces lobby. Gorbachev's opponents were
also critical of his wide powers in foreign affairs, and the fact that he
preferred to operate through state organs rather than Party ones.
Gorbachev had the power to appoint the ministers of defence and
foreign affairs, and had the authority to negotiate and sign treaties. He
appointed a security council in 1990 to advise him on foreign policy, in
place of the Presidential Council. This was seen by many as
concentrating too much power in one person.

6 The Gulf War

In addition to preoccupations with Eastern Europe and problems at home, there were further challenges to be faced abroad. In most instances, Gorbachev faced them realistically.

Iraq invaded Kuwait in August 1990, and the United Nations' response was to assist the victim. Gorbachev faced a dilemma: although Soviet support for Arab radicalism had been less pronounced in recent years, it nevertheless had a long tradition, and there had been a correspondingly cool relationship between the USSR and Israel, one of Iraq's enemies. However, Gorbachev also wanted stability in a volatile region, and he did attempt to initiate better relations with Israel and the less radical Arab states, rather than follow a traditional line. The Soviets were actually in a unique position, having economic and political ties with both Iraq and Kuwait.

Gorbachev had to tread carefully. He supported the UN Security Council resolutions to liberate Kuwait, but there was no question of Soviet military intervention, which would have turned Iraq into an enemy. There was also the problem of divided support at home, where some, like Shevardnadze, were prepared to co-operate with the West against Iraq, whilst some others wanted to support Iraq, although it was the aggressor.

In the event, the Soviet hope that the damage to Iraq by UN intervention would be limited, was realised. The UN operation was confined to the liberation of Kuwait, and the Iraqi regime was not toppled by further Western military operations. However, although this result suited the USSR, it was not the result particularly or solely of its diplomatic efforts.

7 A Global Strategy

Although events in Europe often dominated the headlines, Gorbachev was also active in promoting Soviet interests in other parts of the world, as all Soviet leaders had done. He was particularly keen to extricate the USSR from the long-drawn-out conflict in Afghanistan, an adventure which had imposed a heavy strain on the Soviet economy and had harmed the Soviets psychologically and diplomatically. Continuing intervention did not fit easily with calls for peace and a new world order. In May 1986 Moscow engineered the replacement of the Afghan leader, Karmal, by the more moderate Najibullah Ahmadzai. Soviet troops were withdrawn between 1986 and 1989. It had not been a successful adventure. The Soviet-backed regime only survived after the Red Army was withdrawn because its own enemies were internally divided. The Afghan experience had been a sobering one for the Soviets.

The settlement in Afghanistan helped improve relations with China, which had opposed Soviet intervention. A trade deal had already been struck in July 1985, and a consular agreement in September 1986. The Soviets began to reduce their forces along the Chinese frontier.

Gorbachev maintained close links with India, which he visited in 1986. Elsewhere in Asia, relations with Japan, Thailand, Malaysia, the Philippines, Indonesia and Singapore all improved due to Gorbachev's efforts and protestations of goodwill.

Gorbachev undertook a reassessment of Soviet policy towards developing countries. Soviet activity in some regions had conflicted with other goals, like détente, and had imposed an economic burden. Moscow deliberately began to pay more attention to industrialising capitalist states. Ideological considerations dictated foreign policy less than ever: Gorbachev would deal with countries in a matter calculated to be to the Soviet advantage, whatever the political complexion of the regimes involved.

Gorbachev's foreign policy had had some notable successes. Signing disarmament and arms-control treaties and establishing productive relationships with the USA were themselves notable achievements, particularly given the breakdown of détente at the end of the 1970s. In addition, relations with the old enemy, China, had improved, and with other states, such as Israel, South Africa and the Vatican, all previously hostile to the USSR. Gorbachev deserved much of the credit, for whatever image he projected at home, he was popularly regarded abroad as the dynamic leader of a once-closed society, now seeking to play a responsible world role. However, the historian, Stephen White (in *Gorbachev and After*, 1991), labelled this the 'diplomacy of decline': pointing out the fact that it was the need to reduce military spending which forced the USSR to seek agreements with the West, and which led the Soviets to reduce their strategic forces by a greater proportion than that of the Americans; the fact that the effective end of the Warsaw Pact in 1991 destroyed the Soviet alliance system in Eastern Europe; the fact that the Soviets pulled out of Afghanistan without any assurance that the regime they had backed would survive; the fact that the sphere of influence won in 1945 had been lost; the fact that the countries in which some Soviet influence still remained were amongst the world's poorest. This was hardly success. On the other hand, the world did seem, for at least a time, to be a safer place whilst Gorbachev was in control of the Soviet Union.

Gorbachev's foreign policy did have potentially dangerous domestic implications. The policy was further proof to conservatives that he could not be relied upon to uphold Soviet power and prestige: influence over Eastern Europe and the buffer zone created by Stalin in 1945 were gone. Moreover, troop reductions and withdrawals from Eastern Europe created disruption and threatened unemployment for thousands of army personnel. Not surprisingly, there was a growing body of criticism of Gorbachev from within the military.

Nevertheless, given that the international climate was changing, and that Gorbachev was presiding over a period of destabilisation, with potentially unpredictable and dangerous consequences, his record was an impressive one. It is not surprising that 'Gorbymania', an outbreak of adulation, was heaped upon him by those abroad anxious to see an end to the days of Cold War confrontation. Hence the award of honours culminating in the Nobel Peace Prize in 1990. Gorbachev certainly achieved more success in his foreign than his domestic policy, at least in terms of being rewarded with praise. The world which he left in 1991 was radically different from that of six years before, with the most obvious signs being disarmament agreements, the disbanding of the Warsaw Pact and COMECON, and the at least partial democratisation of Eastern European regimes.

A Superpower in Decline?

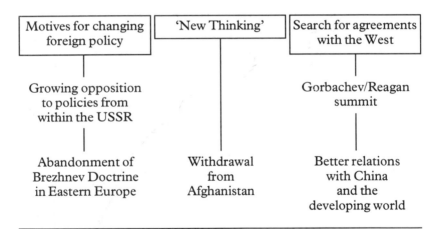

Motives for changing foreign policy	'New Thinking'	Search for agreements with the West
Growing opposition to policies from within the USSR		Gorbachev/Reagan summit
Abandonment of Brezhnev Doctrine in Eastern Europe	Withdrawal from Afghanistan	Better relations with China and the developing world

Making notes on '*'New Thinking': Foreign Policy under Gorbachev'*

The foreign policies of great powers are always significant, but the years between 1985 and 1990 were particularly so for the USSR. When Gorbachev entered office, the USSR, for all its problems, still appeared comfortable in its role as a superpower. But during the next five years, Gorbachev presided over a period of change which witnessed events of great significance, not least of which were the first successes in obtaining a measure of nuclear disarmament, the ending of the Cold War, and the break-up of Soviet-controlled Eastern Europe. All these events were connected, and your notes should contain information on what happened but, equally important, how the events were connected, what Gorbachev was trying to achieve, and the extent to which he fulfilled his

aims. The following headings and subheadings should assist you.
1   The position in 1985
1.1 The difficulties which the USSR faced in its international role at the time of Gorbachev's accession to power in 1985.
2   'New Thinking'
2.1 Why did Gorbachev want to change the thrust of Soviet foreign policy in 1985?
2.2 The meaning and implications of 'New Thinking'
3   Arms control and disarmament
3.1 The achievements and failures of the Gorbachev-Reagan summit
3.2 The extent to which Gorbachev achieved better East-West relations
4   Eastern Europe.
4.1 Gorbachev's attitude towards change in Eastern Europe
4.2 The changes made to the Brezhnev Doctrine
4.3 The significance of Gorbachev's role in events in Eastern Europe.
5   Mounting difficulties
5.1 Why was there opposition to Gorbachev's foreign policy within the USSR?
6   The Gulf War
6.1 Soviet policy during the Gulf War
7   A global strategy
7.1 The Soviet withdrawal from Afghanistan
7.2 Soviet policy towards Asia and the developing world
7.3 Was Soviet foreign policy the 'diplomacy of decline'?
7.4 A summary of Gorbachev's successes and failures in foreign policy

---

Answering essay questions on "New Thinking': Foreign Policy under Gorbachev'

The foreign policy of a country is usually related to its domestic policy, and the connection between the two should have been made clear in this chapter. You may well encounter essay questions which do require an understanding of both aspects. However, the foreign events in which the Soviet Union was involved during this period were so significant that you might have to tackle questions on Gorbachev's foreign policy alone.

The questions may be of a general nature, focusing broadly on the principles of Soviet foreign policy in the second half of the 1980s, and/or its successes and failures. Or they may focus upon a specific aspect: such as Gorbachev's contribution to the ending of the Cold War, or his policy in Eastern Europe. Your answers will often be improved by demonstrating an awareness of the wider context, that is, showing some knowledge of what was happening in other countries which were closely involved with the USSR, as allies, rivals or opponents. You might also need to consider the foreign policies of previous Soviet regimes, and decide how similar or different they were to Gorbachev's. Consider the following questions.

1 To what extent was Gorbachev's 'New Thinking' a radical departure from the foreign policy of his predecessors?
2 How valid is the assertion that the Gorbachev era 'marked the end of the USSR as a superpower on the world stage'?
3 'The most significant feature of Gorbachev's foreign policy was his contribution to the ending of the Cold War.' To what extent do you agree with this assertion?
4 Discuss Gorbachev's role in the break-up of Communist rule in Eastern Europe.

The focus of all these essays is different but, as in earlier chapters, your approach to them should be similar: identify the key words, decide your argument, and plan the themes of each essay.

The key words in question 1 are 'To what extent', 'New Thinking' and 'radical departure'. The question is quite demanding since you need to consider the broader context, which includes the foreign policies of Gorbachev's predecessors. You should certainly consider the policies of Andropov and Chernenko. You *may* wish to consider those of Khrushchev and Stalin, but if you do, identify only the broad themes, and do not get bogged down in detail.

You should then define the principles of Gorbachev's 'New Thinking', as well as the principles of his foreign policy generally, and decide how original they were in order to address the key phrase 'radical departure'. You may decide that some aspects, such as the pursuance of détente, were to some extent only the logical extension of Brezhnev's policies, although more successful because of changed circumstances. You may decide that some policies, such as tolerating and even supporting major political changes in Eastern and central Europe, were very radical. Whatever your line of argument, consider the *motives* and the *results* of Gorbachev's policies, and come to a definite conclusion.

The key words in question 2 are clearly contained in the quotation: 'end of the USSR as a superpower'. It might be useful with this question to consider early on what 'superpower' actually means - not just a country which is large and well armed, but one which has spheres of influence and areas of interest throughout the world, and whose interests have to be considered in any major international developments or initiatives. In this sense, the USSR obviously did remain a superpower, and the negotiations between it and the USA over arms control and disarmament were as important to the rest of the world as to the USSR. The Soviets reduced their commitments elsewhere - for example, withdrawing from Afghanistan and relinquishing their hold on Eastern Europe - and you can argue either that this was an act of statesmanship by Gorbachev, or a sign of weakness. Clearly, when the USSR broke up, Russia lost much of its world power, although it remained an important European power, as well as a nuclear power.

The key words in question 3 are 'significant feature' and 'ending of the Cold War'. This appears to be a more precisely focused essay than questions 1 and 2, although when deciding your line of argument and planning your essay you need to be very clear about your terms of reference. Your answer will probably focus extensively upon the negotiations and agreements between the USSR and the USA after 1985, but you should also remember that the withdrawal from Afghanistan, Soviet support of changes in Eastern Europe, and the very fact of Gorbachev's positive reputation in the West as a realistic, well-intentioned statesman, all contributed to the improving atmosphere in international relations, certainly those between East and West. Therefore this question is, in fact, quite wide-ranging, which is why your planning needs to be precise.

Question 4 has the most precise focus of the four. In some respects this makes your planning more straightforward. You should consider Gorbachev's motives in his dealings with his Warsaw Pact allies, and the actual part he played in events: for example, his refusal to support the hard-liners in East Germany was an important factor in facilitating the changes which ultimately led to German reunification. However, although your line of argument may be clear, in order to do justice to this question, you do require more than a passing knowledge of events in Eastern Europe in the second half of the 1980s, and in particular of the events leading to the break-up of Communist rule in Eastern and central Europe. Remember also that one of the key words in this question is 'discuss'. You are being asked to do much more than *describe* the events, and the fact that the events are relatively recent also makes it more difficult to achieve the perspective which is often a feature of good essays at this level.

Source-based questions on "New Thinking': Foreign Policy under Gorbachev'

1 Anti-Soviet Propaganda
Study carefully the cartoon titled *'Hold It!'* on page 96, and answer the following questions.
a) Explain the message of this Soviet cartoon of 1985. (3 marks)
b) How effective is this cartoon as propaganda? (4 marks)
c) Compare and contrast the message of this cartoon with Gorbachev's 'New Thinking' speech on pages 97-8. How do you account for any differences? (7 marks)
d) What are the uses and limitations of this cartoon as evidence of Cold War attitudes before Gorbachev's 'New Thinking'? (6 marks)

2 Gorbachev's 'New Thinking'
Read carefully the extract from Gorbachev's speech to the Twenty-

seventh Congress of the Communist Party in 1986 on pages 97-8, and then answer the following questions.
a) What reasons did Gorbachev give for a new approach to foreign policy? (3 marks)
b) What did Gorbachev want as the basis for relationships between capitalist and Communist States? (4 marks)
c) What was radically different about the approach in this speech from the Soviet attitude towards the West in Brezhnev's day? (6 marks)
d) Why did this speech arouse opposition in some quarters of the Communist Party? (7 marks)

3 Shevardnadze's Views on Soviet Foreign Policy
Study Shevardnadze's article on page 103, and answer the following questions.
a) What arguments does Shevardnadze use to justify Soviet foreign policy? (4 marks)
b) Explain the reference to 'we permitted changes in Eastern Europe' (lines 11-12). (3 marks)
c) What were the arguments of the critics whom Shevardnadze was attacking? (6 marks)
d) Comment on the tone and effectiveness of this speech. (7 marks)

4 Press Comment on Shevardnadze's Resignation
Study the *Isvestiya* article on page 103, and answer the following questions.
a) What reason is given for Gorbachev's failure to support Shevardnadze? (2 marks)
b) Do you think that *Isvestiya*'s interpretation was correct? (3 marks)
c) What had happened between Gorbachev's 'New Thinking' speech and this article to prompt such pessimism? (8 marks)
d) What is surprising about both this article and Shevardnadze's attitude generally? Does it tell us anything about *glasnost*? (7 marks)

CHAPTER 7

Coup and Counter-coup: The Death of the Soviet Union

1 The New Presidency

By the end of the 1980s it was evident that Gorbachev was committed to more fundamental reform than he had been in 1985. This led to an increasing polarisation between those on the one hand who supported radical changes, and in some respects wanted to push Gorbachev along more quickly than he wished to go, and on the other hand those on the right who thought that he had gone too far already. There were many more who were simply confused, or who were waiting to see what would happen. There were certainly threats on the horizon. As economic problems mounted, and there were increasing manifestations in the republics of nationalist or racial unrest, Gorbachev searched for solutions which would keep the USSR in one piece, allow reform to continue, and maintain stability, preferably under the control of the Communist Party. It was a tall order, and Gorbachev's failure should not have come as a surprise.

In March 1990 an executive presidency was established. Ironically, such a post had been considered after Khrushchev's fall in 1964, and had been rejected then. The intention in 1990 was to provide strong government to fill the vacuum which beckoned after the ending of monolithic Communist control, and to allow the president to act decisively in a crisis. However, Gorbachev still vacillated: he would not stand for popular election to the presidency, nor would he surrender the general secretaryship. It was as if he was still hesitant in his attitude towards reform, and was aware that he no longer had a secure power base. Nor, as yet, was there a new constitution which might give Gorbachev legitimacy. Gorbachev had been elected president by 59 per cent of the Congress votes, but in future the president would be chosen by universal suffrage.

In the meantime, Gorbachev had in theory considerable powers, including the right to nominate candidates for leading state positions, the right to hold up the progress of parliamentary legislation, the right to impose direct presidential rule in a state of emergency, and the right to head a new council of the 15 republican presidents, the effective decision-making body. The president also headed a new security council, responsible for defence.

In December 1990 a cabinet was appointed in place of the Council of Ministers. The first prime minister, Valentin Pavlov, was elected in January 1991, and was accountable to the president. Although Gorbachev was no Stalin, on paper he actually possessed more power than the old dictator had had, and it is not surprising that Yeltsin complained that the USSR might end up with 'an absolutist and authoritarian regime which could ultimately be used to provide a legal pretext for any high-handed act'.

The reality was that, for all his powers on paper, Gorbachev's position was weak compared to that of earlier Soviet leaders. After the Congress of People's Deputies had met in 1989, the individual republics, including the Russian one (the RSFSR), had gone on to hold their own, free elections for their own congresses and supreme soviets in March 1990. Not just Communists, but popular fronts such as *Sajudis* in Lithuania had taken part. In order to compete with the attractions of local nationalist politicians, some of the republican Communist parties became nationalistic in tone themselves. It was clear that local Communist leaders were increasingly ignoring the authority of Gorbachev in Moscow. The Party was certainly threatened, perhaps inevitably so once Article 6 of the constitution guaranteeing it a monopoly of power had been discarded in February 1990.

Forced to look for support, Gorbachev eventually aligned himself with Yeltsin and the radicals who wanted further reform, but then, towards the end of 1991, appointed more hard-liners and appeared to be threatening a return to more authoritarian rule. Technically Gorbachev could be impeached by a two-thirds majority of the Congress, and the Supreme Soviet could force his cabinet to resign. It was unprecedented for a Soviet leader to face a call for his resignation as president (as happened in December 1990), or as general secretary (as the Central Committee requested in April 1991). Otherwise the president could simply be ignored - as some republics did, when their governments would not approve Gorbachev's presidential decrees, and when they bypassed the 1977 constitution by declaring that their own Republican laws took precedence over those of the USSR.

2 The Nationalist Threat

In the mid-1980s, the focus of attention had been on economic and political reform. Few had predicted a resurgence of nationalist and ethnic feeling to the extent that it would threaten the existence of the USSR as a federal state. There had been occasional outbreaks of discontent, which increased as the power of the Communist Party, the force which had effectively kept the Soviet empire together since the immediate post-Revolutionary period, continued to decline. Forty-nine per cent of the Soviet population was non-Russian, according to the 1989 census. Yet from the early days of Communist rule, a deliberate policy of 'Russification' had been employed, partly to dampen down potential unrest and any desire for separatism. Stalin had ruthlessly liquidated or physically transferred whole national groups if he felt that the security of his rule would thereby be strengthened. Under Brezhnev there had been much propagandist talk about the new 'Soviet' citizen, whose admiration for the benefits of Socialism outweighed any separatist instincts. But under Gorbachev old nationalist resentments increasingly came to the fore, and became more and more threatening in the face of the regime's perceived inability to suppress unrest, even had the intention to do so been there.

Gorbachev had at first devoted little attention to nationalist issues, even sounding complacent. In February 1986 he referred to the Soviet nationalities policy as an 'outstanding achievement of Socialism', which had brought great benefits to all the peoples of the USSR. One year later, in his book *Perestroika,* he did admit to problems, although he still described Soviet policy as 'unique'. However, events were soon to change his mind.

The first major outbreak of ethnic discontent under Gorbachev occurred in December 1986. There were riots in Alma-Ata, capital of Kazakhstan. Gorbachev had broken the tradition of having a Kazakh as head of the local Party when he replaced the corrupt Party secretary, Kunaev, with a Russian. The local population expressed their discontent by rioting.

More publicity was given to a demonstration by a group of Crimean Tatars in Red Square in 1987. They were campaigning for a return to the homeland from which they had been evicted by Stalin.

3 Rebellion in the Baltic Republics

More threatening was the discontent in the three Baltic states of Estonia, Latvia and Lithuania. These republics had been forcibly incorporated into the USSR in 1940. The indigenous populations considered themselves as being part of European rather than Russian-Slavic culture; they had a higher standard of living than the Soviets, and they resented increasing Soviet immigration into their territories, as well as their economic exploitation by Moscow. Popular-front organisations and conferences materialised in the three republics in 1988, and demands were made for more sovereignty and restrictions on Soviet rule. When the Estonian parliament ruled that it could override laws issued from Moscow, the Supreme Soviet declared this pronouncement unconstitutional. Concessions only intensified nationalist fervour. The millions of Soviets living inside the Baltic republics were themselves afraid for their future, and made their own claims.

The date 23 August 1989 was the fiftieth anniversary of the signing of the Nazi-Soviet Pact, which had prepared the way for the loss of sovereignty of the Baltic republics. The anniversary was commemorated by a remarkable human chain of two million people, stretching across the territory of the three republics.

Gorbachev now addressed the issues. He told the Nineteenth Party Congress in 1988 that the Soviet government should ensure that nationalist concerns were tackled through popular participation in the governments of the republics, and by strengthening economic links. The Central Committee admitted in August 1989 that nationalist interests had been harmed under Stalin, although it emphasised that Soviets had also suffered. But it still advocated an approach 'free from chauvinism', by which it meant that a reorganised federation rather than a break-up of the Soviet Union was the answer to the problem.

Pro-independence representatives increasingly dominated the supreme soviets within the republics. A clash seemed inevitable when the Lithuanian Supreme Soviet voted to secede from the USSR in March 1990, and then followed this by issuing its own laws and halting conscription into the Soviet army. Moscow declared these actions illegal, sent troops into Lithuania, and imposed an economic embargo.

In May 1990 the Russian Congress of People's Deputies elected its own Supreme Soviet and voted for 'sovereignty', as did the other republics. This meant that Russian laws were to take precedence over Union laws, and for the first time the Russian Republic gained its own Communist Party and institutions such as the KGB, which other republics, but not Russia, had always had. At the meeting of the Russian Supreme Soviet in May 1990, Yeltsin was narrowly elected chairman of this body, despite Gorbachev's attempt to stop this.

Nationalism both inside Russia and the other republics put Gorbachev in a very difficult situation. To avoid a crisis and possible bloodshed, he proposed a new treaty of union, which would establish new procedures for the secession of republics. A draft treaty was prepared in November 1990. Gorbachev was rewarded for his efforts when, in July 1990, the Lithuanian parliament agreed to postpone its declaration of independence, whilst the embargo was lifted. But Estonia and Latvia had meanwhile declared the annexations of 1940 illegal, and so the basic problem of the relationship between the Soviet Union and the three Baltic states was still to be resolved. A similar situation prevailed in Moldavia, also incorporated into the USSR during World War II. The Moldavian Popular Front did secure the resignation of the authoritarian and unpopular Brezhnevite Party secretary in November 1989.

4 The Nationalist Threat Elsewhere

These events threatened the structure of the Soviet Union, but elsewhere more tragic events were unfolding. The region of Nagorno-Karabakh became news in 1988. Although its population was 95 per cent Armenian and Christian, the region had been ceded to Azerbaijan in 1921. The Armenians living there suffered discrimination from the Muslim Azeris, and in February 1988 Azeris rioted in Armenian quarters, killing and looting. The Supreme Soviet attempted to secure better treatment for the Armenians, but would not cede the area to Armenia, so the violence became civil war. Early in 1990

Soviet troops were sent in to impose an uneasy calm.

Georgia also witnessed violence. A popular movement in 1988 and 1989 called for both independence and territorial changes to the republic, and had the support even of many Georgian Communists. The demonstrations of April 1989 turned to tragedy, when the Interior Ministry sent in special troops, and 23 demonstrators were bludgeoned to death with shovels or killed by tear gas. During the resulting state of emergency, Foreign Minister Shevardnadze, himself a Georgian, met the Popular Front leaders. Opposition parties were legalised in time for elections in October 1989. The Georgian Communist Party did badly in the elections, whilst a coalition of pro-independence groups won 54 per cent of the vote. It seemed doubtful whether more bloodshed could be averted as a result.

Less publicised were killings in Ferghana, a region of Uzbekistan. In 1989 there was rioting there between Uzbeks and Meskhatians, an ethnic group that had been moved to Uzbekistan by Stalin in 1944. Once again, special Interior Ministry troops were sent into Ferghanu to restore order.

5 Russian Nationalism: The Threat Within

Therefore throughout the fringes of the Soviet Union, discontent or open violence threatened the break up of the Soviet superpower. But these outbreaks were augmented by developments in the Russian Republic itself. Some Russians resented the fact that they were poorer than some of the other national groups. Some developed a sense of their own ethnic Russian nationalism, which manifested itself in one of two ways: either a feeling that Russia itself would benefit if the other republics broke away; or a determination to enforce Russian control. SOYUZ ('Union') was an alliance of conservative groups, led amongst others by Gorbachev's one-time ally, Ligachev. It demanded a continuation of the Soviet Union. The United Front of Russian Workers protested both against Gorbachev's reforms and the activities of ethnic minorities. The Russian Orthodox Constitutional Monarchists, founded in May 1990, campaigned for Russian dominance over a traditional Russian empire. A month after the emergence of this organisation, the Russian Republic saw the birth of a Russian-only Communist Party. Some intellectuals were attracted to a proposal made in 1990 by Solzhenitsyn for a 'Slavic bloc' of Russia, the Ukraine and Belorussia. The pressures building up on Gorbachev were enormous, and they were coming as much from within Russia as from the more distant parts of the Soviet Union.

6 The Confusion of Political Pluralism

The growth of nationalist and ethnic unrest only added to the domestic pressures which had been steadily building on Gorbachev by the end of the 1980s. It was evident that it was no longer just a question of trying to reverse economic decline, or to determine an appropriate measure of political reform, but that the very survival of the USSR as a political structure might be at stake. Events in late 1989 and 1990 confirmed this trend. Republican and local elections were held, and they demonstrated some differences from the Congress elections. There was a lower turnout, and the contesting parties, including the Communist Party itself, were more organised.

Early in 1990, the Bloc of Democratic Russia was formed. It was an amalgam of over 50 organisations, all committed to some measure of reform, including free elections and the ousting of the Communist Party from a position of prominence. The Bloc put up candidates in the local and regional elections of March 1990, and succeeded in defeating several Communist candidates.

There were also a number of 'centrist' parties, the largest being the Democratic Party. Its platform was a decentralised, democratic Russia within a voluntary union of republics. It copied the organisation of the Soviet Communist Party. In contrast, the Democratic Union was less disciplined, and allowed more individual freedom of action to its members. The Democratic Reform Movement, formally set up in 1991, included some former Gorbachev supporters like Shevardnadze and Alexander Yakovlev. On the left there were various Socialist and 'Green' parties. Further left were the Soviet Communist Party of Bolsheviks, which claimed to have inherited the mantle of the old Communist Party, the Russian Communist Workers' Party, the Socialist Workers' Party, and a Menshevik Party. The People's Party of Free Russia was one of the largest of the new parties.

On the right there were the Bourgeois Democratic Party, the Christian Democrats, and the Liberal Democratic Party, founded in 1990 and led by the extremist, Vladimir Zhirinovsky. One of his policies was the restoration of a Russian state, possibly within the territory of the Soviet Union.

There were also many fringe parties, such as the Kadets (harking back to the pre-Revolutionary period), anarchist groups, a Humour Party, and an Idiots' Party. The features which most of the parties had in common were limited resources, lack of an established base, and a tendency to divide and redivide. Certainly it was impossible to anticipate in advance how individual deputies might vote on many issues. Gorbachev spoke of Russia having become the 'most politicised society in the contemporary world', there being over 500 parties at the Republican level, but the developments were far too new to offer the promise of a stable system of party government. The fledgling parties could not balance a strong executive. By mid-1991 only two parties, including the Communist Party, had registered correctly with the Ministry of Justice, as all new parties were legally obliged to do.

The Communist Party remained powerful. None of the new parties had such assets, including property and money, which had been built up over many years. However, the Communist Party itself no longer presented a united front to the public: it now comprised different groups, taking varied stances on some issues.

7 A Fragile Democracy

Although many citizens initially welcomed the novelty of genuine popular involvement in democratic politics, it soon became a disillusioning experience. Government was not responsive to popular demands, and although deputies themselves could criticise, they could not easily change the system - there was not yet an effective link between those in power and those outside. Democracy was fragile, as the historian, Stephen White, explained:

1 Political reform, by the early 1990s, had certainly succeeded in dismantling a largely Stalinist inheritance, but it had not yet succeeded in replacing it with a viable combination of Leninism and democracy, of central-party control which yet allowed the
5 voters to be sovereign. ... The new representative system, with its inclusion of a range of organised interests, lent itself to the articulation of grievances rather than solutions. Most fundamentally of all, there was an unresolved tension between the 'will of the people', expressed through open and competitive elections, and
10 the 'will of the Party', based ultimately on the doctrine of Marxism-Leninism.
Stephen White, *Gorbachev and After*, Cambridge University Press, 1991, page 67.

Potential political instability was one problem. Equally threatening for Gorbachev personally was the continuing rise to prominence of Boris Yeltsin. The Russian parliament began to pass laws which conflicted with the Union's legislation, and voted to reduce the Russian contribution to the federal treasury.

8 Economic Difficulties and Market Reforms

The economy was also causing increasing concern. The economic programme introduced by Prime Minister Ryzhkov in the late 1980s had failed to arrest the decline in productivity, industrial output, national income and foreign trade. He presented a new programme to the Supreme Soviet in May 1990. It provided for a transition to a 'regulated' market economy in three stages by 1995, with the role of central planning being steadily reduced. It was anticipated that the trend of falling living standards would be reversed after 1993. Stanislav Shatalin, a member of the Presidential Council, put forward a much more radical plan for the transfer of state property into private hands, and the transition to a market economy in 500 days. The Shatalin Plan was rejected on 1 September 1990.

Eventually, a compromise was approved by the Supreme Soviet in October 1990: it provided for a four-stage transition within a 'relatively short time'. The first stage would comprise emergency measures beginning the commercialisation of state enterprises. The second stage would see a relaxation of state control over prices, but a corresponding package of social-security measures to protect vulnerable citizens. The third stage would include changes to the housing market. The fourth stage would see the rouble becoming a fully convertible currency on the world market.

Soviet economic growth, 1986-91
From official Soviet data (%)

	1986-90	1986	1987	1988	1989	1990	1991
Average (plan)							
National income produced	4.2	2.3	1.6	4.4	2.4	-4.0	-15.0
Industrial output	4.6	4.4	3.8	3.9	1.7	-1.2	-7.8
Agricultural output	2.7	5.3	-0.6	1.7	1.3	-2.3	-7.0

There were many voices urging caution, including that of Gorbachev. He had first mentioned 'privatisation' in August 1990, but he also talked about the dangers of exploitation of one class by another under a system of private ownership. He also pointed out that not all market economies were successful. Many officials and ordinary citizens were also cautious, fearing unemployment and continuing shortages. Black-marketeers were the most enthusiastic about the possibilities created by economic uncertainty. Yeltsin insisted that the interests of working people must not be compromised by economic reforms, although he also criticised the existing 'élite structure', which allowed groups to 'wallow in luxury' at the expense of the masses. Gorbachev, as was his wont, tried to hold the middle ground, arguing against full-scale market reforms, and doing little else.

Gorbachev did recognise that he must take some action to resolve such difficult issues, but political concerns placed him in a next-to-impossible position. By conceding to separatist or nationalist demands, he would further alienate the Communist Party and conservatives generally. If he dragged his feet on reform too much, it might be impossible to restrain the radicals and separatists. Gorbachev did not commit himself to one side or another. However, this balancing act was generally regarded not as being statesmanlike, but as a further example of his uncertainty and hesitancy.

Gorbachev did begin to move towards the conservatives, who included Party hard-liners, and brought some of them, like Pugo, Pavlov and Yanaev, into his cabinet. It was this move which prompted the resignation of Shevardnadze and other liberals in December 1990. It also led Yeltsin and the liberal mayors of Moscow and Leningrad, Popov and Sobchak respectively, to resign from the Communist Party and to run for election as democratic candidates.

9 Secession or Union?

Gorbachev had to tackle the problem of the Soviet Union. He acknowledged the republics' right to secede, as was provided for in Article 72 of the constitution, but he appealed for a period of waiting until a proper procedure for secession could be prepared. Unfortunately this proved difficult, and a law passed by the Supreme Soviet in April 1990, which provided for a two-year minimum waiting period between the application for and the granting of secession, was regarded as being unworkable. Difficult issues to be resolved included the situation of those millions of Russians who lived in the non-Russian republics; and what would become of Soviet military bases and equipment - a major issue, since there were, for example, nuclear-weapon installations outside the territory of the Russian Republic. Nor was it just a question of existing republics seceding from the Soviet Union. There were ethnic groups within some republics, such as Poles in Lithuania, who were demanding their own autonomy.

As more and more republics passed laws to override Union legislation, Gorbachev faced a dilemma: should he try to preserve the Union by force, or grant sovereignty to the republics? He may not have fully appreciated the explosive situation: there was one well-publicised occasion when he spoke in Vilnius of the advantages of Lithuania staying in the Soviet Union and integrating the Russian and Lithuanian economies, whilst Lithuanian patriots in the crowd held up the Lithuanian flag and sang patriotic songs. Yeltsin, in contrast, soon realised that he could not dictate policy from the centre, and was prepared to promise full sovereignty to the republics, although his followers still hoped for a loose confederation in which each republic would pursue economic reforms like marketisation at its own pace.

A draft union treaty was published in November 1990, and was immediately condemned for failing to satisfy nationalist demands. It was easy to see why: the treaty insisted on the authority of the Soviet Union's laws, and retained Russian as the official state language. The word 'secession' was not even mentioned, possibly because Gorbachev was attempting to avoid antagonising those elements, particularly within the military and the bureaucracy, which were opposed to the very principle of secession.

10 An Inconclusive Referendum

Gorbachev, as was increasingly becoming the case, was outstripped by events. In February 1991 the Moldavian Supreme Soviet rejected the treaty, and in March the Georgian parliament declared its independence after an overwhelming vote in a Republican referendum in favour of secession. Gorbachev's response was a national referendum on 17 March 1991. The answer 'yes' or 'no' was required to a superficially straightforward, but in reality very complex, question, 'Do you consider it necessary to preserve the Union of Soviet Socialist Republics as a renewed federation of equal sovereign republics, in which the rights and freedoms of an individual of any nationality will be fully guaranteed?'

The referendum was intended to be held throughout the USSR. On the surface the result was a success for Gorbachev, in that a majority voted 'yes' (over 90 per cent voted 'yes' in the central Asian republics, 83 per cent in Belorussia, 70 per cent in the Ukraine, and only 50 per cent in the key cities of Moscow and Leningrad). However, several republics - the three Baltic states, Georgia, Armenia and Moldavia - refused to administer the referendum at all. In Russia, Yeltsin urged the population to treat the referendum as a vote of no confidence in Gorbachev - possibly accounting for the inconclusive result there. Yeltsin added the following question to the referendum in Russia: 'Should Russia elect its own president?' He secured a 'yes' vote.

A crisis point was soon reached. Gorbachev had inadvertently made possible the rise of a separate, non-Communist, Russian government, in parallel with the Soviet one. There were further problems. After the referendum, the six non-participating republics began to co-ordinate their efforts to secede. Gorbachev appeared to be accepting the inevitable, because he announced that he would sign the new Union Treaty with the other nine republics. Yeltsin now pledged his support, after a deal with Gorbachev. In return for Yeltsin's backing for a new Union Treaty, Gorbachev would allow presidential elections to go ahead in Russia, as in the other republics.

Gorbachev appeared to be reverting to reform, yet crucially did not remove the hard-liners from his cabinet. His new stance was probably brought about by a combination of factors. Firstly, he was reluctant to use force. Secondly, there was the fact that the economic situation was deteriorating, with rising inflation, a huge budget deficit, and a collapse of central industrial planning as the republics increasingly went their own way. And thirdly, there was the shock of a series of miners' strikes, the first sign of major public unrest for decades.

However, reform itself was fraught with danger. Gorbachev's idea of a much looser confederation - the republics would control their own internal security, economic resources and media - was unsatisfactory, both to nationalist groups and those hard-line conservatives who were anxious to retain the old federal structure, or something much more like it.

11 Prelude to the Coup

The hostility of conservative groups to Gorbachev had already been confirmed by other events inside the Russian Republic, particularly the loss of the Party's monopoly of power. For all his belief in the Party, Gorbachev had been sensitive to criticisms of its monopolistic position. At the Party conference in June 1988, he had observed that the Party had become involved in too many matters which were not strictly political. By 1990 competitive elections were taking place for some Party offices, in place of the old *Nomenklatura* system, and there was a reduction in the number of Party posts and personnel. There was an increasing polarisation of opinion, with Gorbachev and his supporters calling for a 'Socialist pluralism of opinion', and at the other extreme, organisations such as the anti-Semitic *Pamyat* ('Memory') totally opposed to liberalism and Western-style politics. Gorbachev did not believe that a multiparty system would by itself solve the USSR's problems, but he did believe that 'healthy forces' could co-operate with the Communist Party. His opponent, Yeltsin, went further in criticising the role of the Party, arguing that the latter no longer represented the views of the majority of the population.

The varying political forces were heading for a showdown. The anti-conservative forces had no one leader. There was strong support for Yeltsin in Moscow, and Sobchak in Leningrad. There were liberal-minded people in all institutions, including the KGB and the army, although these bodies tended to be dominated by conservatives. Liberals were disappointed by what they regarded as Gorbachev's perpetual compromises on reform, and similar sentiments were losing him the support of intellectuals. But such critics of Gorbachev lacked a secure institutionalised base of support.

Conservative forces had their weaknesses too, although they did have stronger support in centres of power like the massive Soviet bureaucracy. This support was generated both by conviction and a desire for self-preservation. Conservatives in the Communist Party, and within organisations like the KGB and the army, had been put on the defensive by Gorbachev's reforms in the 1980s: after years of slumber under Brezhnev many had forgotten how to fight for survival. But by the 1990s they were putting themselves and their case forward in the media and in Soviet life generally. In reality, the conservative programme was no more coherent or detailed than that of the liberals, and it appealed to little more than law and order. However, this was a powerful message by

1991, since many Soviet citizens were alarmed at economic develop-ments - the collapse of the rouble, price rises, shortages - and the possible social consequences and threat to public order.

Conservatives knew that if the Union Treaty were implemented, their bases of power in the army, Party and KGB would be fatally weakened, as the centre of political gravity shifted from Moscow to the outlying republics. It was Gorbachev's apparent willingness to see some republics break away from the Soviet Union which decided the plotters, although there were other causes for concern: a week before the coup, Yeltsin banned the formation of Communist Party cells in all Russian enterprises. He also ordered the conversion of many defence plants into factories producing consumer goods.

The new Union Treaty was even more vital for Gorbachev personally. If the USSR broke up, he would have no position, since Yeltsin now controlled Russia, not himself.

The battle lines were being drawn up. Yeltsin campaigned for the Russian presidency in June 1991. His supporters came mainly from the cities, and were often young people who were more prepared for a break with the past and more tolerant of drastic measures to solve Russia's ills. Yeltsin's chief challenger was Gorbachev's long-serving prime minister, Ryzhkov, who argued for moderate reform, but who suffered from his close association with Gorbachev's own discredited reforms. Gorba-chev's own favoured candidate was his economic adviser and recent minister of internal affairs, Vadim Bakatin.

In the June 1991 election Yeltsin won 57.3 per cent of the votes, Ryzhkov 16.85 per cent and Bakatin 3.42 per cent. There were three other candidates: Zhirinovsky, the virulently nationalistic, anti-Semitic and anti-reform candidate polled 7.81 per cent; Aman Tuleev, a Kazakhstani Muslim, polled 6.81 per cent; and General Makashov, standing on a platform combining respect for tradition and the forces of law and order with deference to the Party, polled 3.74 per cent.

Yeltsin's position was clearly strengthened by this result. Gorbachev, although he remained president of the Soviet Union, was correspond-ingly diminished. He had not stood for popular election, although his term of office was not due to expire until March 1995. The vote was widely interpreted as a protest vote against the slow pace and ineffectiveness of Gorbachev's reforms, as well as dissatisfaction with a Congress of People's Deputies packed with conservatives and moderates, which was regarded as being not truly representative of the public mood. If that was Gorbachev's own interpretation, he had little time left in which to do much about it. But probably he was lulled into a false sense of security because, as president, he was to some extent isolated from the pressures of having to fight his corner in the Politburo, as in the old days. Gorbachev was advised instead by the Security Council, founded in December 1990, whose members were appointed by himself, subject to confirmation by the Supreme Soviet; and by the

Council of the Federation, which was interested in inter-ethnic relations. However, Gorbachev's first vice president, Gennadi Yanaev, was to be involved in the forthcoming coup, and there were other powerful forces within the ministries and state committees ready to frustrate Gorbachev's reforms.

12 The August Coup

On 18 August 1991, Gorbachev was on holiday in the Crimea, working on a speech. Days before, one of his advisers, Yakolev, had warned in a television interview that a coup was being prepared by a 'Stalinist grouping' within the Communist Party. However, Gorbachev was still taken by surprise when four delegates arrived from Moscow, placed him under house arrest, and dismantled his telephones in order to prevent his communication with the outside world. Gorbachev refused the delegates' demands either to resign or to sign a decree instituting a state of emergency.

The delegates represented the 'State Emergency Committee', a group of plotters which had assumed power in Moscow. The committee consisted of eight Kremlin conservatives, and they justified their coup in a radio broadcast on 19 August. The committee claimed that *perestroika* had brought the country to a crisis point, in which 'extremist forces' were threatening to seize power. It claimed also that the introduction of market forces had led to both falling living standards and a slide into social malaise. The committee promised to reverse these trends, and declared a state of emergency: meetings were banned, and many newspapers were prevented from publication. Tanks were brought into the centre of Moscow in order to surround the Russian republican parliament building.

The nominal leader of the coup was Gennadi Yanaev, appointed vice president by Gorbachev a year before the coup, as a sop to the conservatives. But the real power among the plotters, all Gorbachev appointees, lay with Vladimir Kryuchkov, chairman of the KGB; Dimitri Yazov, minister of defence; Valentin Pavlov, premier; and Boris Pugo, minister of internal affairs.

The rebels knew that they needed popular support, and counted on the fact that disaffection with the course of events in the USSR would provide this. But Yeltsin, mounting a tank outside the Russian parliament building, and calling for resistance to the coup, inspired enough popular support on his side to enable barricades to be erected to stop further tanks from entering Moscow. Crucially too, there were some younger elements within the army and the KGB, both officers and rank and file, who were prepared to support Yeltsin.

The committee soon realised that it had miscalculated. After wavering, Pavlov, Yazov and Kryuchkov then defected on 20 August. The next day, other members of the committee fled to central Asia. The

Soviet parliament met, and the committee's decrees were cancelled.

The rebel leaders were subsequently arrested. Less than three days after the coup had been launched, Gorbachev was flown back to Moscow from the Crimea as a free man.

Why did the coup fail? In the final analysis, it was a combination of many factors, not just one. Certain individuals deserved credit. Men like Yeltsin in Moscow, Anatolii Sobchak in Leningrad, and Shevardnadze helped to rally support against the coup, both inside Russia and from the outside world. Leningrad in particular held out very strongly against the coup. The biggest mistake of the plotters was their failure to arrest Yeltsin. Also enough ordinary people came out onto the streets to defend the young constitution - not that many, but enough to dissuade both several military units from storming the Russian parliament building, and also the hesitant leaders of the coup from forcibly crushing the resistance or arresting opponents like Yeltsin. Also, ironically, central authority in the USSR had already been effectively destroyed, so that there was little for the coup leaders to take over. The coup came about as a consequence of a crisis in the Soviet economy and political system, and was poorly planned, with few clear objectives.

13 The Aftermath of the Coup

Gorbachev appeared to learn few lessons from the coup. Now, more than ever, he needed to act decisively. But he would not throw in his lot with the liberals and democrats who might have provided him with the following he lacked. Gorbachev seemed out of touch with events. On his return to Moscow, he spent the night in his Kremlin flat, without immediately going to thank Yeltsin and the Russian parliament for securing his release. The day after his return he totally misjudged the prevailing mood by speaking of his continued faith in the Communist Party: 'I will struggle until the very end for the renewal of this Party. I remain a committed Socialist to the depths of my soul', he told a press conference. There were obvious vacancies in the leadership to be filled after the coup, but Gorbachev appointed conservatives who had not opposed the coup, and who may even have collaborated with the plotters.

The proceedings of the Russian parliament on 23 August were televised, to dramatic effect. Gorbachev was present, and was openly criticised for failing to give Yeltsin credit for his release. Yeltsin handed over the minutes of a cabinet meeting which showed that every member of Gorbachev's cabinet, apart from one, had either supported the coup, or had not spoken against it. Only then did a reluctant Gorbachev agree that the entire government should resign.

Gorbachev's power was effectively destroyed. Likewise, the remains of the old Soviet establishment were discredited, and anti-Soviet forces, both nationalistic and democratic, received at least a temporary boost.

Yeltsin made new appointments, and suspended the operations of the Communist Party in the Russian Federation on 23 August. A few days later, the Supreme Soviet decreed the same for the entire USSR. All the financial assets of the Communist Party were frozen, and its buildings were furthermore seized.

Those conservatives who had been trying to reverse the political and economic reforms of the previous six years were themselves discredited by the coup, not just by the efforts of people like Yeltsin, and even less so by Gorbachev, but by their own hesitation and incompetence. Nevertheless, the coup was only an interlude in a continuing catalogue of difficulties. The 1991 harvest failed, and the spectre of famine threatened to become a reality. News of continuing ethnic discontent hit the headlines, and the USSR appeared to be on the verge of breaking up. The only political figure who emerged notably stronger from the coup was Boris Yeltsin, and he himself was about to inherit many of the problems which had been plaguing Gorbachev.

14 The End of the USSR

Ironically, by trying to prevent the signing of the new Union Treaty, the plotters of August 1991 hastened the destruction of the USSR. Some republics (the Baltic states, Moldavia, the Ukraine, and Armenia) had opposed the coup. Some, like Tajikistan, had supported it or had been noncommittal. Some minorities, as well as Russian settlers in other republics, had supported the coup. The coup showed that all of the USSR's problems were bound up in some way or another with the nationality issue.

Soon the various republics declared their independence from the old Soviet Union, and applied to join the United Nations as separate states. Lithuania had actually declared its independence in March 1990, and during the coup Estonia and Latvia had done likewise. They were soon followed by the Ukraine and other republics. It was the secession of the Ukraine in December 1991 that killed off any remaining hopes of retaining a loosely federated Soviet Union. Several of the new states created their own armies. In December 1991 Russia, the Ukraine and Belorussia formed the Commonwealth of Independent States (CIS). Most of the other republics soon joined. However, it was a very loose organisation, with no parliament or presidency. The structure of the USSR, as originally conceived in 1922, was destroyed.

The CIS members agreed to honour existing international agreements signed by the old USSR, and they agreed on the principle of unitary control of nuclear weapons. More complex were the economic arrangements, since in the USSR there had been a division of labour between the republics - for example, Russia had provided other republics with oil and gas, whilst cotton was supplied by the Asian republics. There were also the ethnic problems, the rights of minorities, and territorial disputes to be considered.

Although the USSR had collapsed as a federal institution, not everything had changed. Most of the economy and social provision were still in state hands. But Yeltsin, one month older than Gorbachev, was Russia's new leader. He embarked on a struggle with his conservative parliament. In April 1993 he won a 58.7 per cent majority in a referendum calling for confidence in his presidency. But he was to face mounting popular pressure whilst trying to cope with an ailing economy and growing political disaffection. Democracy was in a precarious state. Ominously, the Communist Party of the Soviet Union was allowed to re-form in 1993, and was to become the largest of the political parties.

Gorbachev was clearly redundant. He resigned on 25 December 1991. He left office with a staff of 20, two cars and 4,000 roubles. Whilst not immediately sinking into obscurity, the focus shifted very much to Yeltsin, the Russian president. A new era was beginning, not just in Russia, but in all the former states of the old Soviet Union.

Making notes on 'Coup and Counter-coup: The Death of the Soviet Union'

When reading this chapter, you should consider the growing problems of the USSR as Gorbachev's policies ran into difficulties; the causes and events of the August coup, and its aftermath, including the break-up of the Soviet Union. The following headings, subheadings and questions should help you when you make notes.

1   The new presidency
1.1 The executive presidency
2   The nationalist threat
2.1 Gorbachev's attitude towards nationalism
2.2 What outbreaks of nationalist discontent were there in the late 1980s? How serious were they?
2.3 Russian attitudes towards nationalism
3   Rebellion in the Baltic republics
4   The nationalist threat elsewhere
4.1 What outbreaks of nationalist discontent were there? How serious were they?
5   Russian nationalism: the threat within
5.1 What evidence was there of Russian nationalism?
6   The confusion of political pluralism
6.1 Political groupings
7   A fragile democracy
8   Economic difficulties and market reforms
9   Secession or union?
10   An inconclusive referendum
11   Prelude to the coup

Answering essay questions on 'Coup and Counter-Coup: The Death of the Soviet Union'

In this final section, there are essays which cover a much broader span of Soviet history, in fact, the whole period from 1964 to 1991. At first sight, these questions may seem more daunting than some of those in previous chapters. However, you should adopt the same approach as before: identify key words, plan your arguments and the main body of your essay, and bring together your arguments in a conclusion. Then you should be able to deal competently with the questions. It may be that you will go into less detail about individual events or aspects than with some earlier essays, and it is even more important to keep the thread of your argument to the fore. But the key is always to take each question on its own merits.

The following examples are all variants on the theme of continuity and change in the generation between the fall of Khrushchev and the break-up of the USSR under Gorbachev:

1   'A period of stagnation followed by reform.' How far is this a valid analysis of Soviet political and economic life between 1964 and 1991?
2   Why did the Soviet Union break up in the early 1990s?
3   'It was not the conservatism of Brezhnev that destroyed the Soviet Union, but the radicalism of his successors.' To what extent is this a valid analysis of the period 1964-91 in Soviet history?
4   Did the condition of the Soviet people improve or deteriorate during the era of Brezhnev and Gorbachev, 1964-91?

In essay number 1 the key words are in the quotation: 'stagnation followed by reform'; and also in the phrase 'political and economic life'. You are not obliged to give equal weight to political and economic factors in your answer, but you should certainly give attention to both. As with all such quotations, you do not have to agree with the sentiments, but any comments you make on the quotation should not be generalisations, but arguments backed up by evidence. You will need to describe and analyse the main features of the political and economic systems during these years - and give some attention to the Andropov-Chernenko period, where appropriate, as well as to the regimes of Brezhnev and Gorbachev. Consider those elements which changed little or not at all, and those which changed considerably. Under 'political', you should consider political structures, the role of the Communist Party, and the move towards some pluralism under Gorbachev. Under 'economic', you should consider the structure of the command economy, and the attempts to tinker with it and change it under *perestroika*. You are not obliged to go into great detail about the *effectiveness* or otherwise of the reforms, although this will certainly form part of your answer, particularly in the conclusion.

Essay number 2 is deceptively simple, and the key word is 'Why'. Although you will probably start your essay with a brief description of the break-up of the USSR, the main theme of your essay should be an analysis of why it broke up. 'Causation' questions like this one are often best approached by considering short-term and long-term causes. Your line of argument might be that it was Gorbachev's reforms which both raised expectations and fuelled fears, and which began the process which led to events such as nationalist outbreaks, political uncertainty and the coup, and eventually to the break-up of the Soviet Union. However, a more thoughtful answer will also look back beyond Gorbachev and will consider the strains and pressures, particularly economic, within the Soviet Union, to which Gorbachev was responding. Then you can address issues such as: was the break-up inevitable even before Gorbachev came to power, and did his policies simply alter the timescale of the process? Or was the break-up basically Gorbachev's responsibility? Clearly there is no simple answer, which is why in your planning you should be very clear on your line of argument and decide your approach on the appropriate evidence.

There are several key words and phrases in essay number 3: 'conservatism of Brezhnev', 'radicalism of his successors', and 'To what extent'. The timescale of the question is clear. You should decide early on whether you agree with all the implications of the quotation. Whilst it would be legitimate to bring in some aspects of foreign policy and defence (since, for example, heavy spending on defence and global commitments contributed to internal strains), the bulk of your answer will probably be devoted to domestic political and economic issues. You may well agree, and produce evidence to support the argument, that Brezhnev was basically conservative in approach, which was indeed a major factor in his success in retaining power. You might argue that, in the case of his successors, certainly Andropov and Gorbachev, the picture is less clear cut: you may take the line that the changes they introduced were not radical, in the sense that these two leaders expected several of the key elements of the Communist system to stay in place. On the other hand, you may wish to argue that it was the changes that they instituted, whether very radical or not, which brought about, or at least hastened, the break-up of the USSR. You will need to think through your arguments very carefully in your planning of the essay.

Essay number 4 is quite demanding. The key words are 'condition of the Soviet people' and 'improve or deteriorate'. The timescale is clear, because it is given to you. However, the phrase 'condition of the people' is to be treated with care, because it can lead you into simplistic generalisations. Decide early on which factors contributed to the 'condition of the people' - political, economic and social - and decide how much weight you intend to give to each. Also, what is meant by 'the people'? You might argue that different groups had different expectations, and were affected differently by the regimes' policies. For example, you may wish to consider gender differences, differences between Party and non-Party members, between young and old, between citizens of Russia and the other republics. Clearly, people belonged at the same time to different groupings, but equally clearly some people benefited to a different extent at different times. Having considered these complex issues, you need to try to reach an overall judgment on the 'condition of the people' in 1964 and a generation later, and compare the two situations. To some extent, your answer will also depend upon whether you consider material conditions or other considerations were more important to individuals: did, for example, developing political freedoms compensate for growing economic uncertainties?

In all these essays, you must think clearly and decide on your line of approach before planning your introductions, main bodies of the essays, and your conclusions.

CHAPTER 8

The Post-Gorbachev Era

Gorbachev's resignation and the break-up of the USSR were events of considerable significance, not just for the countries of the former Soviet Union, but also for the wider world.

1 Russia and the World: A New Role?

Gorbachev left Russia and the former countries of the Union facing a very uncertain future, and there was considerable speculation, both within and outside Russia, about the likely course of events.

The place of Russia on the international stage was one immediate issue. Clearly, with the demise of the old Soviet Union, Russia could no longer aspire to the influential superpower role it had once enjoyed, albeit at a cost, in Brezhnev's day. Russia simply did not have the economic or political clout to exercise influence throughout the world. But what influence would Russia exert on international relations in the future? The break-up of the Soviet Union was seen as the event which signified the end of the Cold War, the situation of ideological and physical confrontation that had dominated East-West international relations for more than 40 years. It had also created a power vacuum in international relations. It was not a situation that the Russian government relished. Russia alone of all the former states of the Soviet Union could realistically aspire to a significant role beyond its borders; and the Russian government expected to be involved in decision-making in areas in which it had traditionally had interests, for example, the former Yugoslavia, which was in the throes of civil war.

However, there was no consensus on the exact nature of Russia's future role. Many Russians felt humiliated at the loss of their country's superpower status. There were those among them, extreme nationalists, prepared to feed on this feeling and other discontents to further their own political ends. There were other, more outward-looking, Russians, Gorbachev among them, who talked not of nationalism but of a 'common European home', and possibly even of integration into an expanded European Union. Would either of these views, or indeed others, triumph?

There were more immediate issues to be resolved: territorial claims on Russia's neighbours such as the Ukraine, and questions such as how would the former Soviet navy be divided amongst the successor states?

Would the ending of the Cold War and the break-up of the Warsaw Pact lead to a reappraisal of NATO? How would relations between Russia and its former client states in the Soviet Eastern European bloc develop? Would the West offer material support to Russia in its desire to see further internal reform, and would continuing support be conditional on those reforms being implemented? How extensive would

Russian influence be in the post-Cold War world? The answers to all these questions were very uncertain in 1991.

2 New States and New Problems

The rise of nationalist feelings in Russia fuelled apprehension amongst ethnic groups, both inside and outside Russia, particularly since there were politicians prepared to exploit these sentiments in order to oppose reform or to serve other ends.

The situation of the republics of the former Soviet Union posed particular problems. With the controlling hand of the Communist Party gone, local rivalries and hatreds came to the fore. Ethnic quarrels spilled over into civil war. Fighting broke out in several areas, including Georgia. Within Russian sovereign territory, the regions of Chechenya and Tatarstan refused to sign a 1992 federation treaty. Meanwhile, Latvia, Estonia and Lithuania looked increasingly to Western Europe as a focus for their future hopes. The Asian republics were more inward looking, and had their own problems to contend with, particularly since their economies, manipulated and specialised to serve the interests of the Soviet Union as a whole, were too unbalanced to meet the requirements of independent nations.

A major question in 1991 was: how would the smaller or less-developed republics cope in the post-Soviet world, and would they maintain constructive and mutually beneficial relations with their old Russian masters? Although 11 of the 15 former republics formed the Commonwealth of Independent States, and agreed to encourage trade between themselves, each was a sovereign state. Disputes between members broke out almost immediately: amongst the issues involved were the prices of exports and the control of nuclear weapons.

3 Democracy or Authoritarianism?

The political future of Russia in 1991 seemed clouded. Gorbachev had undermined the old, monolithic, one-party system. *Glasnost* and the encouraging of political pluralism had begun a process of democratisation. It was a process applauded in many quarters in the West, where democracy had long-established roots. However, it was a new concept in the states of the former USSR. Russia itself had experienced only a brief period of democratic hopes between the two revolutions of 1917. For centuries before 1917, and for decades afterwards, the Russians had experienced authoritarian government. Democratic attitudes could not be implanted overnight. There was no tradition of public political debate or of political parties, other than the Communists, with established procedures for mobilising grass-roots support. The many new political parties that had emerged towards the end of the 1980s had no traditions, often no coherent policies or party discipline, and they presented a confusing picture to an electorate never before faced with genuine choice.

Politicians themselves were treading new ground. Gorbachev had encouraged political pluralism, whilst assuming that the Communist Party would retain a significant and possibly even controlling role. Was this a contradiction? Gorbachev himself had begun to drag his feet on the subject of political change, whilst trying to avoid the two extremes of radical reform and reaction. His attempts to hold the middle ground of compromise had simply fuelled uncertainty and dissatisfaction.

A similar dilemma faced Gorbachev's successor in Russia, Boris Yeltsin. Yeltsin had helped to destroy the influence of the Communist Party, and had stood out against the anti-Gorbachev plotters, but after 1991 he began to display his own authoritarian tendencies when challenged. Yeltsin was a fighter in difficult circumstances, and circumstances became increasingly difficult. President Yeltsin was soon at odds with his own conservative parliament. In March 1993 that parliament tried to strip Yeltsin of his powers. A referendum was held in the following month, and it provided Yeltsin with a vote of confidence, but then he had to survive an attempted coup against him. In addition, his drastic economic measures, aimed at reversing a deteriorating economic situation, brought him growing unpopularity. Ominously for the future, he began to argue for more and more executive powers in order to increase his own authority.

The issue was not just one of Yeltsin's personal prestige or even survival. If Yeltsin were defeated by a democratic process, or forcibly overthrown, there would be no leader with enough general support to succeed him and govern by consensus. The alternatives to Yeltsin were likely to be an unwieldy coalition, the emergence of a nationalist leader feeding on discontent, a military coup, or the re-emergence of a Communist Party. The latter would at least be able to point to a tradition of order and predictability which Russians understood. Perhaps not surprisingly, given the volatile situation, support for the Communists did begin to grow again.

Russia in 1991 was facing a situation which has afflicted many political systems once they have begun to reform from within: once the hold on the reins has been relaxed, it is difficult to retain control of events, particularly when there has been no tradition of political consensus supported by genuine popular participation. Democracy could only be nurtured gradually, not imposed. In a situation of political fluidity, would pressure groups seize the initiative? A lot would depend, as always, on the economy. If the economy improved, there would be less disatisfaction on which extremists could feed. Could Yeltsin and the new political system survive long enough to enjoy the fruits of reform? Were there enough citizens committed to reform and capable of making the informed choices which would benefit themselves and their country?

4 The Economy and Society: Hope or Disillusionment?

Economic and social developments were part of the key to Russia's future, and also the future of the other republics. After all, it had been concern about the stagnating Soviet economy which had prompted *perestroika* in the first place. However, the economic reforms of the mid- and late 1980s had appeared to lack conviction, consistency and coherence. In 1991 the territories of the old Soviet Union were still suffering from the legacy of the Stalinist system of crude economic planning based on central direction and the diversion of massive resources into the arms race and heavy industry. In part this had been due to the Soviet attempt to maintain its superpower status.

Glasnost had been an integral part of *perestroika*. Genuine economic reform was impractical without encouraging openness and initiative. However, the short-term results of Gorbachev's economic measures had been disappointing, and there was little confidence that the long-term results would be any better. Ordinary citizens had gained some personal freedoms, but faced difficult material conditions: employment was no longer guaranteed, and a reduction in state controls and subsidies had a significant effect on prices and the cost of living. Once the Soviet state had provided a basic level of material security. That prop was disappearing. Whilst there was a generation able and anxious to take advantage of the opportunities opened up by privatisation to make good, there were more who fell behind or who simply did not understand the implications of market economics. Would these people lose faith in discredited reforms and turn their back on the new political system too? Would an individual or movement promising stability and material security prove more attractive?

Russia was in.a potentially stronger position than the other republics. It could supply its own energy and food needs, and had over 75 per cent of the former Soviet Union's industry. It was rich in natural resources. In contrast, for example, the Baltic republics were dependent on Russia for their energy supplies. Nevertheless, the Russian economic outlook was very uncertain in 1991.

Certainly, social and economic issues were coming increasingly to the fore, and whilst they had always been present in the Soviet system, they were now more highlighted and openly discussed in the glare of the media. Organised crime was on the increase. Inflation approached 1000 per cent a year. Could the benefits of capitalist market economics be introduced without its vices as well? Could democracy and Socialism be reconciled? Economic concerns fuelled a growing discontentment with politics and politicians - a dangerous situation in any society, but particularly in one in which the old structures were being dismantled.

5 Change and Stability: An Uncertain Future

How to reconcile change and stability in a volatile political culture was the greatest challenge facing the states of the old Soviet Union. Gorbachev had failed to manage the process successfully. As his adviser Alexander Yakolev had succinctly put it: 'We are trying to sail a ship and simultaneously rebuild it. We don't have a spare ship to step into for a moment and sail'. Gorbachev had been a product of the Soviet system, and he could not resolve the dilemma of being both a reformer and a political operator within the old system. He tried hard, but perhaps he could not rise above the limitations of the ideology on which he had been nurtured. Could any one person hope to solve Russia's problems? New leaders were certainly required to carry the republics forward into the post-Communist future, but the problems that they faced were at least as great as those which had confronted their failed predecessors. Could the new leaders hope to succeed?

Glossary

Apparatchik	Normally a Party worker, a member of the 'apparatus'
CC	The Central Committee of the Communist Party
CIS	Commonwealth of Independent States
COMECON	The Council for Mutual Economic Assistance (sometimes called CMEA)
CP or CPSU	The Communist Party of the Soviet Union
Détente	A relaxation of tension during the Cold War
General secretary	(or first secretary, 1953-66) the leading figure in the CP
Glasnost	'Openness'
Gosplan	The State Planning Committee
Gulag	Chief Administration of Corrective Labour Camps
KGB	Committee for State Security (or secret police)
Kolkhoz	collective farm
Komsomol	Young Communist League
MTS	Machine-tractor station
NEP	New economic policy (1921-28)
Nomenklatura	List of important positions to which Party members were promoted
Pamyat	('Memory') an anti-Semitic nationalist organisation
Perestroika	'Restructuring'
Plenum	A full meeting of the CC
Politburo	(The Presidium, 1952-66), the Political Bureau or decision-making body of the CC
RSFSR	Russian Soviet Federative Socialist Republic
Samizdat	'Unofficial' or underground publications
Supreme Soviet	The all-union legislative body

Further Reading

In order to succeed at an advanced level of study, it is important that you read reasonably widely. You are not expected to read large numbers of specialist books, but you should consult at least a few. There are many excellent books available on the period of Soviet history up to, and including, Khrushchev, but there are far fewer written for students at this level on the period under Brezhnev and beyond. The following titles are amongst the most useful for students studying Soviet history between 1964 and 1991.

G. Hosking's *A History of the Soviet Union* (Fontana, 1985) is readable and covers the Brezhnev period quite effectively.

J. Keep's *The Last of the Empires. A History of the Soviet Union 1945-1991* (OUP, 1995) is recent, detailed and readable.

The remaining titles are more specialist studies on particular aspects or periods of Soviet history in the era of Brezhnev and Gorbachev, and should be of use to all students studying at an advanced level.

R. Edmonds' *Soviet Foreign Policy: The Brezhnev Years* (OUP, 1983) is a detailed description and analysis of Soviet foreign policy in the 1960s and 1970s.

J. Steele's *The Limits of Soviet Power: The Kremlin's Foreign Policy - Brezhnev to Chernenko* (Penguin, 1985) is useful in giving a different and more radical interpretation of Soviet foreign policy.

M. McCauley's *The Soviet Union under Gorbachev* (Macmillan, 1987) is a collection of detailed essays on the politics and economics of the first three years of Gorbachev's time in power.

A. Nove's *An Economic History of the USSR* (Penguin 3rd ed., 1990) is authoritative on economic aspects.

M. Walker's *The Waking Giant: The Soviet Union under Gorbachev* (Abacus, 1987) is the work of a newspaper correspondent in Moscow, and deals with the rise of Gorbachev and the impact of his policies of *glasnost* and *perestroika*.

Stephen White has written two very useful books on the Gorbachev era. His *USSR - A Superpower in Transition* (Pulse Publications, 1989) deals with social, cultural and economic issues, as well as with the politics of the Gorbachev era. His more difficult, but rewarding, book *After Gorbachev* (CUP, 1993) is very authoritative in dealing both with Gorbachev in power and the break-up of the USSR.

J. Laver's *The USSR, 1945-1990* (Hodder and Stoughton - *History at Source* series, 1991) is a collection of written and visual sources on domestic affairs and foreign policy, many from the period 1964-90. Also included are examination questions and plenty of practical advice for students.

Index